DICTATORS' DINNERS

DICTATORS' DINNERS

A BAD TASTE GUIDE TO ENTERTAINING TYRANTS

GILGAMESH
PUBLISHING

Published in 2014 by Gilgamesh Publishing Ltd.
29 Sedgeford Road London W12 0NA
Tel: +44 (0)7753 745252
Email: info@gilgamesh-publishing.co.uk
www.gilgamesh-publishing.co.uk

© Victoria Clark and Melissa Scott 2015

Designed by Carter Wong Design Ltd.

ISBN: 978-1908531-48-3

CIP Data: A catalogue for this book is available from the British Library.

CONTENTS

1.   EUROPE   8

Joseph Stalin, USSR   10

Benito Mussolini, Italy   16

Adolf Hitler, Germany   22

Antonio Salazar, Portugal   28

Francisco Franco, Spain   34

Josip Broz Tito, Yugoslavia   40

Erich Honecker, German Democratic Republic   46

Nicolae Ceaușescu, Romania   52

2.   MIDDLE EAST   58

Saddam Hussein, Iraq   60

Muammar Gaddafi, Libya   66

3.   AFRICA   72

Hastings Kamuzu Banda, Malawi   74

Jean Bedel Bokassa, Central African Republic   80

Idi Amin, Uganda   86

Mobutu Sese Seko, Congo   92

Mengistu Haile Mariam, Ethiopia   98

Francisco Macias Nguema, Equatorial Guinea   104

Kwame Nkrumah, Ghana   110

4.   ASIA   116

Mao Zedong, China   118

Ferdinand Marcos, Philippines   124

Pol Pot, Cambodia   130

Saparmurat Niyazov, Turkmenistan   136

Kim Jong-Il, North Korea   142

5.   AMERICAS   148

Rafael Trujillo, Dominican Republic   150

François 'Papa Doc' Duvalier, Haiti   156

Alfredo Stroessner, Paraguay   162

Fidel Castro, Cuba   168

FOREWORD

For the first time, we subject the worst dictators of the 20th century to collective culinary scrutiny....

Who would have thought that vegetarian Hitler wolfed down baby pigeon stuffed with tongue and liver, or that Mussolini craved nothing more than bowls of raw garlic? Could anyone have guessed that Malawi's austere Hastings Banda kept crispy fried worms in his trouser pockets or that Uganda's Idi Amin – strongly suspected of cannibal tendencies – devoured forty oranges a day? Did Communist Fidel Castro really lecture people on how to grill lobster, and Pol Pot dine on cobra stew?

In this novel blend of history, photo album and recipe book readers will find the culinary concept usefully expanded; here are startling insights into the dictators' table-talk and manners, gastro-intestinal issues, domestic arrangements, addictions, infirmities and food policies. Where humanly possible we have supplied a recipe for the dictator's favourite dish; where impossible, we have made educated guesses or resorted to lateral thinking.

Our survey is far from exhaustive, of course. Albania's Enver Hoxha, Chile's Augusto Pinochet, Vietnam's Ho Chi Minh and Egypt's Gamal Abdul Nasser, are obvious absences. In general, we have made our selection on the basis of variety and interest and judged them to qualify as dictators if they rose to power by way of a coup d'état or overruled their constitutions to retain power. All but two of our subjects are now dead, and the remainder – Cuba's Fidel Castro and Ethiopia's Mengistu – are out of power.

We very much hope this book will amuse and inform readers, but also acquaint them with some exotic cuisine and, by the by, remind them just how thin the line between man and monster can be. As our endpapers testify, in their heydays, our dictators were all courted and feted by more respectable leaders.

Victoria Clark and Melissa Scott
November 2014

EUROPE

JOSEPH STALIN

1878 – 1953

Stalin first encountered Lenin's writings while still a schoolboy, studying for the Orthodox priesthood at a seminary in the Georgian capital, Tblisi. Pockmarked by smallpox and with one arm shorter than the other following a horse and cart accident, he was clever enough to rob banks for Lenin's Marxist underground movement and ambitious enough to rise swiftly to the top of the organisation which seized power in the Russian Revolution of 1917.

In spite of Lenin's reservations about his protégé's ambition and ruthlessness, Stalin succeeded him in 1924. He proceeded to purge potential rivals and terrorise everyone else with the Great Famine of 1932-3, imprisonment in Siberian labour camps known as the Gulag and deportation of entire ethnic minorities to the Central Asian republics.

On his orders and at the cost of some 22 million lives, Russia was transformed into an industrial power strong enough to withstand invasion by Nazi Germany in June 1941 and so end the war in Europe. Stalin's USSR emerged from the conflict as one of the world's two superpowers, in a position to oversee the consolidation of Communist regimes in Eastern and Central Europe as well as the building of a Soviet nuclear weapon. Nostalgia for his rule is widespread in today's Russia.

The variety and quality of the food served at Stalin's table had everything to do with his Georgian roots.

Georgian cuisine features walnuts, garlic, plums and pomegranates and its wines are among the finest in the region. Georgia has a strong tradition of hospitality. Feasting was so integral to the court of Georgian Tsar Stalin that his successor, Nikita Khrushchev, once remarked: 'I don't think there has ever been a leader of comparable responsibilities who wasted more time than Stalin did just sitting around the dinner table eating and drinking.'

But was he wasting his time? Delicious Georgian meals were ideal settings for the sort of lethal power-play that sustained him in power. A Georgian toastmaker – a *tamada* – at first controls his fellow diners' access to alcohol by the length of his opening speech, and thereafter by ensuring that more

and more is drunk to avoid injury to the host's pride. **Drinking games – 'Guess the Temperature' was one of Stalin's favourites – reduced many guests to his Kuntsevo dacha outside Moscow or one of his many summer residences to staggering, incontinent wrecks.**

Yugoslavia's Tito wound up vomiting into his jacket sleeve and Czechoslovakia's Klement Gottwald found himself begging Stalin to allow his country to join the USSR. Khrushchev himself wet his bed after one marathon dinner. In the summer of 1942, famously hard-headed Winston Churchill downed a skinful of Stalin's favourite Khvanchkara wine, a semi-sweet red, and was complaining of a headache by 3am.

What Stalin referred to as 'a bite to eat' often involved a six-hour dinner – preferably cooked by his favourite chef, President Vladimir Putin's grandfather, Spiridon Putin – with no way out until 5 in the morning. He bullied and bored the company with repeated anecdotes and set a tone so delinquently boorish it disgusted even his own daughter, Svetlana. Hurling

tomatoes at a fellow Politburo member, flicking bread pellets and puerile teasing were all permitted. Singing and dancing were compulsory.

Rumours that Stalin died by poisoning persist, but an average evening of Georgian-style feasting in the company of his closest cronies would surely have sufficed to provoke a huge stroke in the 75 year-old tyrant.

SATSIVI

Serves 6

The name translates as 'that which has cooled down' because the dish is served cold or just slightly warm, as a starter.

1.5kg/ 3lbs 3oz whole chicken

700g/ 1lb 5oz walnuts

5 medium onions

4 cloves of garlic

2 tbsp white wine vinegar

1 tsp dried coriander

1 tsp blue fenugreek

1 heaped tsp dried marigold

1 heaped tsp dried red pepper

½ tsp cinnamon

5 crushed cloves

Salt

Fill a pan with 2 litres of water, and add the chicken. Heat until parboiled, then remove the chicken and place on a roasting tray, using some of the surface oil from the boiled water to baste the chicken. Do not discard the boiled water. Roast the chicken at 180°C/350°F.

Cut the roasted chicken into serving portion-size pieces.

Finely chop the onions and fry in more of the surface oil from the boiled chicken for 6 to 7 minutes.

Transfer the onions to mixing bowl and smooth to a paste with a hand blender. Add the onion paste to the boiled chicken water.

Grind the walnuts finely, into a mixing bowl Add the coriander, fenugreek, marigold, cinnamon and cloves. Mix by hand.

Crush the red pepper, garlic and salt in a pestle and mortar, before adding this mix and the vinegar to the walnut mix.

Gradually add the rest of the boiled chicken water to the mixture until it has a smooth consistency.

Hold the sieve over the pot used for boiling the chicken and pour the mixture through, discarding any large particles left in the sieve.

Add the chicken pieces to the mix and bring it to the boil, before removing from the heat.

Allow to cool before serving.

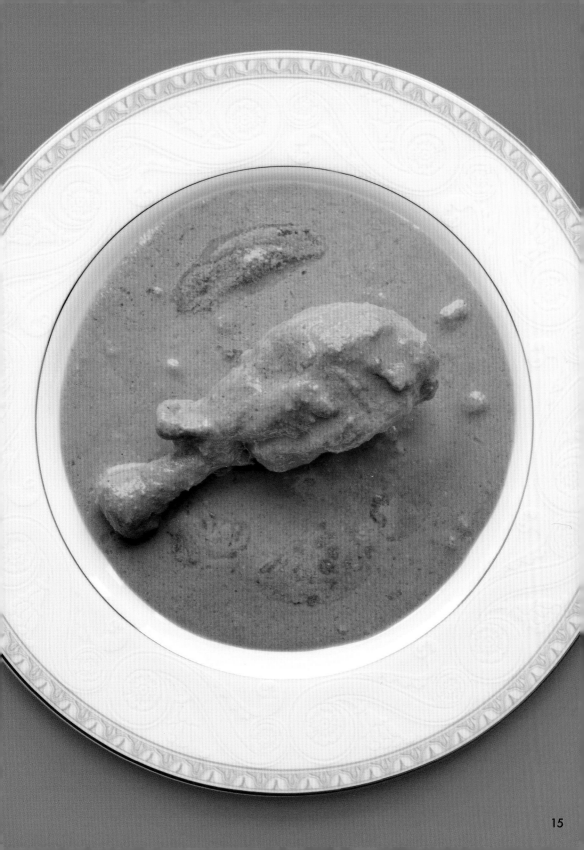

BENITO MUSSOLINI

1883 – 1945

Delinquent eldest son of a socialist blacksmith and a schoolteacher from Emilia Romagna, boastful and bullfrog-like, Benito Mussolini learned his socialism while a poor migrant worker in Switzerland and, merging it with nationalism, established his Fascist Party in 1919.

Flanked by his squads of storm-trooping Black Shirts, most of them unemployed veterans of World War One, he looked to Italy's king and most Italians like the only force capable of rescuing Italy from mounting chaos. By 1922, he was Italy's youngest prime minister ever and he had established a dictatorship and proclaimed himself Il Duce (the leader) by 1925. He then set about returning Italians to their roots as citizens of ancient imperial Rome with a foreign policy to match.

After re-asserting colonial rule over Libya, he conquered Abyssinia (today's Ethiopia), annexed Albania and had allied Italy with his fellow fascist's Nazi Germany and imperial Japan by the start of World War Two. But, ailing and badly weakened he proved unable to resist the Allied invasion of Italy in 1943. Deposed, arrested and imprisoned, he escaped with German assistance and led a remnant puppet state for a time but he was re-captured in 1945, near Lake Como and strung up from a lamp-post in Milan, alongside his mistress, Clara Petacci.

Strutting, chin jutting and bombastic *Il Duce* may have been, but a glutton he certainly was not.

A favourite dish was a simple salad of roughly chopped raw garlic, dressed with oil and lemon, which he maintained was good for his heart. 'He used to eat a whole bowl of it,' his wife Rachele once fondly confided to the family cook, 'I couldn't go anywhere near him after that. At night I'd leave him to sleep alone in our room and take refuge in one of the children's rooms!'

Unmoved by his nation's now world-famous cuisine and wines, Benito Mussolini greatly admired both Mahatma Gandhi and George Bernard Shaw for their vegetarianism and had given up alcohol entirely by the time he was forty.

Pasta interested him only in so far as it was made from wheat, the production of which needed boosting in the mid 1920s.

The battle for bigger wheat harvests was an early fascist success; production went up by a third. Using the Latin word for soldier, he motivated all farmers growing wheat by granting them all the ancient Roman-sounding title, *velites*. In 1928 he penned a little poem in praise of bread, a more usefully proletarian food even than pasta:

Love bread, heart of the house,
Scent of the canteen, jewel of the hearth.
Respect bread, sweat of the brow.
Pride of work, poem of sacrifice...
Don't waste bread, wealth of the nation,
God's sweetest gift
Holiest reward of human fatigue.

However pressing affairs of state or extra-marital love, Mussolini ate his meals at home, with Rachele and their five children. Always punctual, he liked everyone else to be seated and ready by the time he arrived to preside over a long oval table. He encouraged stimulating discussion and the airing of opinions. In her book 'At Table with the Duce', Maria Scicolone, the family cook, has recalled how he welcomed the inclusion of grapefruit in his diet after Italy's colonisation of Libya, how it provoked a lengthy and stimulating table discussion about the geographical origins of tomatoes and other vegetables.

When pressed for his view on national cuisines, Mussolini reportedly divulged that French cooking was worthless and Italian the best in the world; in top place was Emilia-Romagnan cuisine, then Tuscan, then Roman, in his view. He was a fast eater and, exactly like his friend Herr Hitler, greatly resented having to attend long, formal meals at the royal palace as the guest of Italy's King Victor Emmanuel III.

Others have recalled his lamentable table manners, 'the incredibly creative gyrations he engaged in when using his knife and fork' as a young man. He quickly learned better once in power, but never forgot a deprived boyhood. A few vegetables with a few drops of olive oil and a slice of bread had been all he could expect for lunch when staying with his maternal grandmother.

As early as 1925, only three years into his rule, he was diagnosed as suffering from a duodenal ulcer, but Italian doctors mistreated the condition, recommending he drank over a litre of milk a day. A more able physician examined him in 1943 and pronounced him insomniac, anaemic and acutely constipated, with an enlarged liver, heightened blood sugar and a deformed colon. A revised diet that included rabbit and chicken brought about a startling improvement. However, Mussolini could not eat mashed potatoes because he claimed they gave him a headache.

Mussolini did not like meat but could be tempted by a good piece of veal, marinated in various herbs, including marjoram from the garden. The Mussolini clan all adored a good ciambellone for pudding.

CIAMBELLONE

Serves 6

A pudding recipe for Ciambellone was a firm family favourite.

500g/ 18oz flour

3 eggs

150g/ 5oz sugar

240ml/ 1 cup of milk

120ml/ ½ cup of olive oil

Grated peel of 1 lemon

240ml/ 1 cup of Mistra (aniseed liqueur)

Sachet of pudding yeast

Preheat the oven to 180°C/355°F.

In a large bowl whip the eggs, sugar, milk and oil together. Add the grated lemon and liqueur. Gradually mix in flour and yeast

Grease and flour a pudding mould. Pour in the mixture and sprinkle with sugar.

Place in the oven and leave for 30 minutes (without opening oven).

After half an hour use a toothpick to check if the ciambellone is cooked. If the toothpick comes out wet continue cooking until it is nicely dry in the middle and golden on top.

Allow to cool and serve in slices.

DICTATORS' DINNERS

ADOLF HITLER

1889 – 1945

A penniless watercolourist from the provincial Austrian town of Linz, Adolf Hitler was a decorated veteran of World War One who owed his rise to the fragile Weimar Republic's fatal combination of national humiliation and hyper-inflation. Hitler successfully peddled a promise to avenge Germany's defeat and restore first her economic, then her military strength.

The German system of election by proportional representation eased his rise via the ballot box, and an impressive economic recovery and a boldly expansionist foreign policy characterised the first five years of his regime. By the time he invaded Poland in 1939 he had re-militarised the Rhineland and annexed Austria and Czechoslovakia's Sudetenland on the pretext of protecting the rights of all German-speakers everywhere and gaining Germany some Lebensraum (living space). When he moved on to attack Poland, Britain and France declared war.

In the six years that followed Nazi forces overran most of mainland Europe, systematically exterminating the continent's Jews as they went, and anyone else Hitler had designated Untermenschen (sub-humans) in his Nazi bible, Mein Kampf. The Luftwaffe's bombing of England failed, but Stalin's Soviet Union with its inexhaustible manpower and unspeakable winters defeated Nazism. In April 1945 Hitler committed suicide in his Berlin bunker rather than risk capture by the advancing Soviet troops.

Long touted as the world's most infamous vegetarian, Adolf Hitler was not, in fact, a fanatical purist in this area.

On several occasions in the 1930s he wolfed down fledgling pigeon stuffed with tongue, liver and pistachio nuts and, at least once, reportedly remarked that that here was 'nothing better than a liver dumpling'.

His vegetarianism has been attributed to a tender concern for the humbler species of the animal kingdom. Certainly, the Nazi regime fretted about the rights of lobsters imprisoned in restaurant aquaria, and went so far as to ban foie gras. On the other hand, an essay titled *Heroism and Christianity*, by Hitler's favourite composer and fellow anti-Semite, Richard Wagner, suggests that his vegetarianism had a crucial part to play in his planned purification of the Volk. Wagner's treatise argued that humans had been natural vegetarians until forced into carnivorous ways after some tragically careless cross-breeding with cannibal ancient Jews. Hitler once explicitly acknowledged his debt to Wagner: 'I don't eat meat largely because of what Wagner says on the subject.'

Largely, but perhaps not entirely, a third, more banal motivation for the Fuhrer's vegetarianism was reportedly his belief that a meat-free diet would curb his chronic flatulence and constipation, conditions for which he took as many as 28 different drugs on the orders of his quack physician. Along with large doses of amphetamines he needed to keep him from collapse – explained away as vitamins to anyone who dared ask – Dr Theodor Morrell injected the Nazi leader with substances such as an essence of Bulgarian peasant's faeces, arsenic-based rat poison in the form of Dr Koester's Anti-Gas Pills and deadly nightshade.

Hitler feared poisoning by food much more than by medicine, however. The only one of his team of 15 food-tasters to survive the war, Margit Wolf, lived in East Prussia near the Fuhrer's Wolf's Lair headquarters and recalls the SS driving her to the nearest town where all the great leader's food was prepared. The superior quality of the meals struck her: 'There was asparagus in season, with Hollandaise sauce, vegetable broths with little semolina dumplings, roasted red peppers, rice, salads and vegetable stews'. Only after a period of 45 minutes had elapsed without any taster dropping dead was a dish deemed safe for transportation to Hitler's table.

The topic of vegetarianism was sometimes aired at that table. Meat-eating guests could be revolted into laying down their cutlery by the Fuhrer's detailed description of a visit to a Ukrainian slaughterhouse, for example. Their leader's deplorable table manners might have had much the same effect.

A soldier who shared the last few weeks of Hitler's life in the bunker and ate with him on some thirty occasions recalled the spectacle of him wolfing down his food in a mechanical way, and the way he bit his nails at table, and ran his index finger back and forth under his nose, and stuffed himself with cake.

No one was allowed to smoke at table on account of his susceptibility to laryngitis. **By the final months of the war Hitler's chronically dysfunctional digestion had reduced him to a nursery diet of mashed potato and clear broth.**

It was a very far cry from the elaborately haute cuisine Petits Poussins à la Hambourg, which a British chef named Dione Lucas remembered serving him in a Hamburg hotel in the early 1930s. 'I do not mean to spoil your appetite for stuffed squab, but you might be interested to know' she told readers of her Gourmet Cooking School Cookbook (1964), 'that it was a great favourite with Mr Hitler who dined at the hotel often.'

PETITS POUSSINS À LA HAMBOURG

Serves 6

This recipe features squabs, baby pigeons. Ask your butcher to split the skin down the back of each and remove their ribs, breastbone and backbone, leaving thighs and wing bones in. Keep the other bones, and the livers.

6 squabs

17 chicken livers

butter

½ bottle of Calvados

¼ tsp of chopped garlic

12 mushrooms

1 lemon

170g/ 6oz cooked and shredded tongue

3 tbsp blanched pistachio nuts

3 green apples

plain flour

granulated sugar

560ml/ 1 pint single cream

2 tbsp chopped truffle

2 tbsp chopped fresh tarragon

salt and pepper

Stuffing

Lay the spatch-cocked squabs on a wooden board.

In a frying pan, brown 12 chicken livers and the squab liver in 2 tbsp of very hot melted butter. Flambé in 6 tbsp of Calvados. Remove from pan.

Fry 12 sliced mushrooms and a quarter tsp of chopped garlic in 3 oz of melted butter. Cook for 2 minutes, adding 1 ½ tsp of lemon juice and seasoning. Add 170g of shredded, cooked tongue and 3 tbsp of blanched pistachio nuts and the carefully sliced cooked livers.

Peel, core and slice in ¼ inch thick pieces 3 green apples and dry the slices well with a paper towel before sautéing them in hot butter and a little sugar. The slices shouldn't get too soft.

Shape the squabs around a spoon or two of stuffing and sew up carefully, making sure that the skin is safely closed. Tie up in parcels with string.

(At this point you can place the squabs in the fridge and finish the dish at a later date.)

Roasting Meat

Preheat oven to 190°C/375°F

Place squabs in heavy sauté pan, in 4 oz of hot melted butter. Cover with lid to brown slowly.

Flambé in ¾ of a cup of Calvados. Place pan on top shelf of oven for 45-50 minutes. Baste twice, adding more Calvados if necessary.

When cooked, remove squabs from pan, remove string, discard bones and keep juices for the gravy.

Gravy

Add the lightly whipped cream one tsp at a time. Add 2 tbsp of finely chopped truffle. Add 2 tbsp of finely chopped tarragon.

DICTATORS' DINNERS

ANTONIO SALAZAR

1889 - 1970

A professor of economics at Coimbra University, Salazar took some persuading by Portugal's army to leave his ivory tower and become prime minister in 1932. He remained in power until his death in 1970, never marrying, shunning celebrity and adoring crowds, devoting himself utterly to his work.

More like a religious ascetic than a dictator of his era, he earned the respect of leaders all over the world, although his Estado Novo government was deeply conservative, firmly rooted in Catholic social doctrine and ultimately authoritarian. Liberal individualism was anathema to Salazar. One visit to Portugal's parliament while a young man had been enough for him; he hated the disorder of democracy. But his antipathy towards Adolf Hitler on account of his paganism and racism proved equally strong in the late 1930s. Portugal remained neutral throughout World War Two and helpful towards Jewish refugees.

Critics allege that Salazar's policies led to an economic and social stagnation that fuelled mass emigration in the 1950s and 60s and needlessly impoverished Portugal, but he remains a national treasure in the eyes of his own people. In a 2013 television poll 41% of viewers voted him the greatest Portuguese that ever lived, greater even than Henry the Navigator.

Salazar always believed that his devotion to Portugal required him to forego a wife and family. Like everything else about his everyday existence therefore, his nutrition was managed by a housekeeper known to the nation as Dona Maria.

Dona Maria's biographer describes her as the 'authentic interpreter of the president's capricious palate' but also, less admiringly, as 'a common person, rude, disciplined and a little brutal' who relieved him of any need for direct contact with those whose lives he governed. Isolated himself, he was busy isolating his country from the storms sweeping the rest of Europe and the wider world, and always ate alone.

He hated Dona Maria using the telephone, even when she was noting down recipes for dishes to make him, and his views on women would make any western woman today, feminist or not, blanch: **'How can I stop a wave of feminine independence crashing upon our world?'** he mused, 'They do not understand that happiness is reached by renouncing rather than having,' he reasoned, 'the great nations should set the example, keeping women in the home.' His lonely meals were ferried from the kitchen via a hoist and pulley system to the first floor of his home, into a little pantry beside the dining room, where Dona Maria put the finishing touches to everything he ate.

Salazar's approach to food and drink was ascetic in the extreme; the exact cost of every meal interested him. **He breakfasted on barley coffee or tea served with plain toast, no milk or butter. Lunch would start with a soup made from ground up turkey or fish bones, or simple cabbage. His favourite dish was grilled sardines and black-eyed beans because it reminded him of an impoverished childhood in which he had had to share a single sardine with a sibling.**

A visiting female French journalist, for whom he clearly had a soft spot, was nevertheless forbidden either to smoke or drink a post-prandial coffee at his table.

An avalanche of foodstuffs from his adoring people – biscuits, eggs, nuts, fruits and fish – helped Dona Maria keep within her tight housekeeping budget.

31

SARDINAS GRELHADAS COM FEIJAO FRADE

Serves 4

(Grilled sardines with black-eyed beans)

Beans

300g/ 10oz black-eyed beans, soaked for 2 hours

1 peeled garlic clove

½ a red onion, finely chopped

60ml/ 2fl.oz extra virgin olive oil

1 tbsp red wine vinegar

A large bunch of flat leaf parsley, finely chopped

Sardines

12-16 whole fresh sardines – scaled, cleaned and rinsed

400g/ 8oz peeled, seeded and diced tomatoes

180ml/ 6fl.oz extra virgin olive oil

60g/2oz of pitted, chopped Kalamata olives

2 tbsp fresh basil

2 tbsp minced shallot

1 tbsp minced garlic

60ml/ 2fl.oz plus 1 tbsp freshly squeezed lemon juice

Sea salt and black pepper

1 lemon, sliced not too thin

4 cherry tomatoes halved

Beans

Drain the beans and rinse under running water.

Place them in a large saucepan with garlic and enough water to cover, and bring to the boil. Reduce heat and cook for another 25 minutes until tender. Drain, remove and reserve the garlic clove. Set aside to cool.

Finely chop reserved garlic clove and place in bowl with beans, onion, oil and vinegar, season with salt and pepper and scatter with parsley. Serve with lemon wedges.

Sardines

Lay the sardines on a piece of dry kitchen towel and gently roll up to remove all excess moisture. Refrigerate until ready to use.

Preheat grill to high.

In medium-sized mixing bowl combine tomatoes, ½ cup of olive oil, olives, parsley, basil, shallot and garlic. Add 1 tbsp lemon juice, 1 tsp of salt and ½ tsp of pepper. Mix well and set aside at room temperature until ready to serve sardines.

Put sardines on a baking tray and drizzle over ¼ cup of olive oil. Coat the fish by turning them over and season with salt and pepper.

Put on grill and cook for 2-3 minutes undisturbed, until the skin is lightly charred and crispy. Turn them and cook for another 2-3 minutes; the fish will turn easily once the skin has crisped.

While the fish are cooking brush the lemon slices and tomato halves lightly with oil and season with salt and pepper and place on grill for about 2 minutes on both sides – until softened.

Place tomato mixture on serving dish, with sardines arranged on top. Add more salt and pepper and a drizzle of remaining lemon juice and olive oil. Place lemon slices and tomato on top and serve.

FRANCISCO FRANCO

1892 – 1975

Diminutive youngest son of a feckless Galician naval officer and a strictly pious mother, Francisco Franco was short on inches but long on romantic ambition. He joined the army and covered himself with glory, earning a reputation for quasi-supernatural feats of bravery and luck in combat in Spanish North Africa.

The removal of the rigidly Catholic monarchy and the rise to power of Spain's socialist and atheist Popular Front in 1931 shocked him into plotting a military coup that unleashed three years of catastrophic civil war. Franco's fascist Falangist forces relied on military assistance from their fellow anti-Bolshevik, Adolf Hitler; the aeroplanes that bombed Guernica in 1937 – an episode made unforgettable by Picasso's painting – were German. Two years later Franco emerged victorious, as Spain's El Caudillo de la Ultima Cruzada y de la Hispanidad (Leader of the Last Crusade and Spanishness).

He would rule Spain for more than forty years, keeping her out of World War Two while repaying his debt to Hitler and the German people in food that his own people needed. Conservative, rigidly Catholic and utterly lacking in charisma in his middle and late years, Franco provided for the orderly restoration of the monarchy by naming Prince Juan Carlos as his eventual successor.

'Let them eat dolphin sandwiches, made with fish-meal bread!' Luckily for the dolphins, General Francisco Franco's pettishly Marie Antoinette-ish solution to the famine ravaging his country in the 1940s was never implemented.

While keeping Spain out of World War Two, Europe's most diminutive but durable dictator saw fit to starve his countrymen by exporting most of Spain's agricultural produce to Nazi Germany. By 1950 Spanish meat consumption was only half what it had been in the mid-1920s. Bread consumption had halved since the outbreak of the Civil War in 1936.

Franco's admiration for Hitler did not extend as far as vegetarianism. Rather the reverse; always suspicious of what he perceived to be vegetarians' natural inclination towards socialism, he was a devoted carnivore with a hearty appetite and a deadly serious attitude towards food. While still a common or garden army general, he had a soldier executed for throwing food at an officer.

His idea of rest and recreation from the trials of dictating to Spaniards often involved celebrating his virility by slaughtering the biggest mammals he could find on land and at sea. By the time he reached late middle

age he bore a closer resemblance to his admirer, the macho sportsman novelist Ernest Hemingway, than to Queen Marie Antoinette. **'The pursuit of large tuna was becoming a passion,'** notes a biographer, proceeding to enumerate some bumper culls of Spanish wildlife.
In the summer of 1958, in Asturias, he followed up a gigantic haul of over 60 salmon – some of them weighing over 30 pounds – with a 20-ton whale. The following year he shot 5000 partridges and almost a decade later, at the venerable age of 76, he succeeded in landing a whale weighing 22 tons.

Indefatigable in the wild while stalking his prey, he demonstrated extraordinary stamina in government too. **In his prime, a normal working day began at 7am and ended at midnight; he did not start taking siestas until well into his seventies. Nine hour-long cabinet meetings were feats of endurance for all concerned, during which he reportedly went without breaks for either refreshment or excretion.** In his later years, however, hunting, shooting or deep sea fishing expeditions ate into this punishing work schedule, often extending from Saturday through Monday. Anyone seeking to influence Franco hastened to cultivate a raging bloodlust of their own.

Franco's culinary legacy to his people remains disputed. Many Spaniards believe the reason why Madrid restaurants always include paella on their Thursday menus is down to *El Caudillo*'s habit of taking his lunch in town on that day of the week; no self-respecting restauranteur could have risked the shame of having to tell the great leader that his favourite dish was off the menu.

No one can be sure that paella was Franco's favourite dish, but certainly a good paella's surf and turf components – prawns and chicken – would have chimed with Franco's sporting interests.

PAELLA GALLEGA

Serves 8

Galicia's paella owes its seafood to Galicia's maritime location. The dish was originally Valencian; its name derives from the Valencian-Catalan word for a pan.

¼ **onion, chopped**

¼ **red pepper, finely chopped**

¼ **yellow pepper, finely chopped**

3-4 sliced white mushrooms

1 chorizo

500g/ 1lb10oz chicken thighs or breasts, trimmed of fat and cut into small chunks

500g/ 1lb10oz whole king prawns

500g / 1lb10oz of mixed clams and mussels

¼ **tsp of saffron**

1 tbsp chopped tomatoes or tomato puree

800g/ 1lb8oz medium or short grain rice

olive oil

480ml/ 1pint dry white wine

2litres/ 4pints of chicken stock

100g/ 4oz of frozen green peas

Put a good splash of olive oil in paella pan.

Sauté onions, peppers, mushrooms and chorizo on a medium heat for short time.

Turn up heat and add chicken, spreading all over the pan and turning so equally cooked all over.

Drain away excess oil. Turn up heat and add white wine to meat Sprinkle pinch of saffron and stir. Spread rice over the pan and add chicken stock, evenly. Add chopped tomatoes or purée, and stir.

Cook for 10 minutes.

Add clams and mussels, evenly spread. Cook on low heat for 10-15 minutes – the rice needs a total of 30 minutes.

When the stock has almost been soaked up by the rice add the prawns and sprinkle the peas on top.

Place it in the oven at 180°C/350°F for the last 10 minutes.

Remove from the oven and cover with a clean cloth for a few minutes to allow the flavours to infuse.

Place the paella in the centre of the table and serve.

JOSIP BROZ TITO

1892 – 1980

Of humble peasant Croat origins, Josip Broz Tito fought in the Austro-Hungarian army on the Russian front in World War One. Captured and imprisoned in the Urals, he participated in the Russian Revolution before returning to fledgling Yugoslavia as a devout Communist. In World War Two he emerged as the charismatic and highly effective leader of Yugoslavia's excellent Partisan resistance movement.

From 1943 until his death in 1987 he was the undisputed supreme leader of his country, Marshal of Yugoslavia. His insistence on the slogan 'brotherhood and unity' for Yugoslavia's six republics held the historically fractious region together. His defiance of Stalin, his image as a bon viveur and his leading role in the Non-Aligned Movement – a 'third way' that aimed at maintaining a healthy distance from both world superpowers – won him international respect. So did his promotion of an economic boom in his country in the 1960s and '70s and Yugoslavs' freedom from the travel restrictions operating elsewhere in the Eastern Bloc.

A New York Times obituary noted that his Yugoslavia had been 'a bright spot amid the general grayness of Eastern Europe'. His fourth and last wife, Jovanka, made a glamorous but feisty first lady from whom he was quietly divorced in the late 1970s.

The most oxymoronic of Eastern Bloc dictators, Tito was 'a Communist with style'.

In a lifetime of fine dining and travel that took him everywhere but Australia, he is reported to have baulked at only one culinary adventure: a dish of sparrow. He didn't think he had it in him, he told his Chinese hosts, to eat 'the proletarian of the bird kingdom'.

Tito turned fine dining – often aboard his luxury yacht, the Galeb (Seagull) while sailing down the fabulous Croatian coast – into a crucial plank of a buccaneering foreign policy. Hundreds of heads of state and celebrities were recipients of his hospitality; Sophia Loren even lent a hand in the kitchen. An official visit from Mali's president involved a dinner aboard the Galeb with conversation about whether or not the Sahara Desert

belonged to France, to the accompaniment of Paganini and fireworks twinning Mali's and Yugoslavia's national emblems.

In private, Tito's culinary tastes harked back to his lowly childhood in the hills of Zagorje where the fine dining comprised a *struklji* or a bite of smoked pig's head. The latter dish features in an improving tale all Yugoslavs learned. Once, when Tito's parents had gone out leaving him in charge of siblings who were wailing with hunger, little Josip remembered that the attic contained a smoked pig's head intended as a Christmas treat. Trembling with terror, he fetched it down, boiled it up with some flour and fed it to his brothers and sisters. Before long, the little ones were writhing in agony over their too-rich food. When the Broz parents finally returned, they were filled with pity and brave little Tito-to-be escaped a thrashing.

Presented with a suckling pig in his old age, Tito would apparently waste no time in 'cutting off a slice of warm fat'. His favourite breakfast was buckwheat porridge laced with bacon or some pork crackling, and a helping of fried egg whites.

Whether fancy or folksy, all Tito's meals were checked by a Russian-trained lab technician. Only foods marked 'A-U' – analysed-usable – were served.

His taste in wines was patriotic: Slovenian Cviceck or a Kutjevo rosé.

STRUKLJI

Serves 6

Versatile as well as filling, struklji can be baked or boiled and served as an accompaniment to a heavy meat stew, as a main course with a salad, or dusted with sugar, as a dessert.

Dough

500g/ 1lb1oz plain flour

1 egg

2 tbsp sunflower oil

1 tbsp vinegar

250ml/ 9fl.oz lukewarm water

pinch of salt

Filling

4 eggs

1 tbsp melted butter

600g/ 1lb3oz cheese – ricotta, dry curd cottage cheese or feta work well

100ml/ 4fl.oz sour cream or plain yoghurt

2 tsp salt

On a clean work surface use your fingers to combine the flour, egg, oil, vinegar, salt and water into a dough.

Knead for approximately 10 minutes, until soft and stretchy. Then divide into 3 equal chunks.

Brush a plate with oil and places the 3 chunks on it. Brush the sides and tops of the chunks with oil too. Cover with foil and leave to rest for 30 minutes.

Prepare the filing by stirring 1 tbsp of melted butter into the cheese. Add the eggs, salt and sour cream or yoghurt. Mix well.

Preheat the oven to 200°C/390°F. Sprinkle flour onto a clean tablecloth which you smooth out with your fingers. Take first chunk of dough and roll into a rectangle, using a rolling pin. Then, use your fingertips to stretch it a bit further.

Drizzle melted butter all over the stretched dough. Next, using about a quarter of the cheese mix, smooth it all over the dough, leaving a 2 cm border on all sides.

Fold the stretched dough over and begin to roll horizontally. When you get to the final 2 cm brush the dough with melted butter, to make a seal.

Use the edge of a plate to cut the roll into chunks about 7 cm long. The plate's edge will seal the parcels so that the filing doesn't spill out. Repeat the process for other 2 chunks of dough, using a quarter of the filling in each one, leaving a quarter of the mix.

Grease a baking tray well. Arrange the struklji in rows so they're touching each other. Spread the rest of the cheese mix on top.

Bake for approximately 45 minutes. Serve warm.

ERICH HONECKER

1912 – 1994

Last but one leader of the DDR, otherwise known as Communist East Germany, Erich Honecker is a hot contender for the prize for failing to notice the winds of change that were blowing in the region in the late 1980s. He was once described as having an 'almost sinister, unstudied immovability'.

To a hint from the USSR's Mikhail Gorbachev that he might like to consider a few adjustments, he famously claimed: 'We have done our perestroika. We have nothing to restructure.' Son of a coal miner from the Saar region, Honecker was a Communist activist by the age of 14 and spent the duration of World War Two in a Nazi jail. Freed by advancing Soviet troops in 1945, he resumed his climbing of the German Communist Party ladder, taking charge of the building of the Berlin Wall in 1961. Responsible for the order to shoot anyone trying to cross the wall, he presided over the deaths of 125 East Germans.

Despite his lugubrious demeanour, he married three times – first his prison warden and then two fellow party activists. He and his third wife, Margot, were serially unfaithful to each other but never divorced. He was ousted in October 1989, although his trial for human rights abuses was abandoned due to terminal illness.

'Whoever knows me knows that I drank much water and little wine,' said Honecker, precisely recalling his nutritional regime while in power, 'every morning I ate one or two rolls with only butter and honey. For lunch-time I was in the Central Committee; there I had either sausage with mashed potatoes, macaroni with bacon or goulash...'

Seized by Ostalgie – a widespread nostalgia for the old East Germany – since the end of the Cold War, Berliners have opened a new museum to the now defunct state, complete with a café proudly serving up Honecker's absolutely favourite meal: yet another variation on a stolid culinary theme, smoked pork with pickled cabbage. Perhaps Honecker could risk a less than healthy diet having given up both smoking and alcohol on his accession to power in 1971, after his Soviet-backed ousting of his predecessor.

When it came to food, Communist East Germany was more thorough than most of the Eastern Bloc in its determination to resist polluting Western influences. Cooking shows on television promoted specialities of neighbouring fraternal socialist states, rather than Italian or French cuisine.

Authentically German hamburgers and frankfurters were stripped of any West German and American associations at the Gastronomic Rationalisation and Research Centre by being re-named, *Grilletta* and *Ketwurst* respectively; an East German pizza was known as a *Krusta*. Instead of Coca Cola, East Germans happily knocked back their less sweet and slightly more viscous *Vita Cola*, production of which halted when the Berlin Wall came down, but restarted in 1994.

Any shortfall in the national meat supply was concealed by a compensating promotion of East German-caught herring and a slogan such as **'Two fish each week keep you healthy, slim and young!'** No fish at all however, for a banquet for the first Western European leader to grace the GDR with a state visit, the Finnish president. Thanks to the recent publication of an Ostalgic cook-book titled *Essen wie Erich* (Eat like Erich) we know precisely what was served: **fruit cocktail with curry-flavoured whipped cream, mushroom-flecked guinea-fowl broth, lamb medallions on a bed of artichokes, pork rolls stuffed with apples and raisins and a red wine jelly for dessert.**

KASSELER MIT SAUERKRAUT

Serves 6

Kasseler are pork steaks, lightly smoked and then soaked in a salt brine solution, (I cup of salt to 4 ½ litres of water) – are available from German delicatessens, and only need to be heated through. Sauerkraut, pickled cabbage, is available in jars from large supermarkets.

100g/ 4oz butter

I small onion, finely chopped

700g jar of sauerkraut

500ml/ I pint of a dry white wine, Riesling for example

8 lightly crushed juniper berries

6 Kasseler steaks

Melt 80 g/ 3oz of butter in heavy-bottomed pan over a medium heat.

Add onion and cook, stirring for 3 minutes.

Add sauerkraut, wine and juniper berries, and bring to boil.

Reduce heat to low and cook, stirring occasionally, for 45 minutes, until almost all the liquid has evaporated. Add water if it's too dry, and salt and pepper.

Heat 20g / Ioz of butter in frying pan over a medium heat, and cook the pork steaks for five minutes on each side.

NICOLAE CEAUSESCU

1918 – 1989

Trained as a humble cobbler, Ceausescu rose up through the ranks of the post-war Romanian Communist party to become the country's leader in 1965. By the mid 1970s he had decided that the country must be as free as possible from Moscow's influence. His much lauded 'maverick' status within the Eastern Bloc won him many friends in the West, especially after he opposed the Soviet invasion of Czechoslovakia in 1968.

A decade later, Queen Elizabeth hosted him and his wife, the stern chemist, Elena, on a state visit. By then he had decided to run the country like a rural smallholding; Romania had to be self-sufficient and repay all her foreign debts. By the 1980s his boasted Epoca de Aur (Golden Era) was a Securitate-policed reign of terror and mass deprivation. Plans to destroy Romania's villages caused Europe-wide disquiet; even Prince Charles voiced his outrage.

Mrs Ceausescu's pretentious tastes and dubious academic qualifications won her even more enemies than her husband. In December 1989 the loathed couple were removed in a coup staged by Communist Party reformers under cover of a popular uprising that had begun among members of the ethnic Hungarian community. Footage of the Ceausescus' execution by firing squad was beamed around the world on Christmas Day.

Nicolae Ceausescu was a simple, healthy eater.

A vegetarian lasagna – layers of spinach and pancake, topped off with an egg beaten into some soured cream – was one of his favourite dishes. *Piftie din Crap Romanesc* (Romanian-style Carp in Aspic) was another, but a simple tomato, onion and feta salad, served with a steak also found favour, especially in his later years. The family cook has recalled how a recipe for tomato soup with home-made noodles earned his high praise: **'Look what a sweet-smelling something we have here! Let's see if it tastes as it good as it smells!'**

Disapproving of any waste, Ceausescu never lost his liking for *Tocanita de Pui cu Mamaliguta*, a stew involving the slow-cooking of an entire chicken – head, wings and feet included – or for the yellow *Galbeni de Odobesti* wine he drank with it. Elena especially enjoyed *Coliva*, a traditional Romanian

funeral food made of barley, washed down with Cordon Rouge champagne.

As his oppressive reign progressed and he compared notes with fellow dictators, his terror of poisoning intensified; Fidel Castro confided that an attempt had once been made to poison him by way of his boots. By the 1980s Ceausescu's fear was a full-blown paranoia. He never wore the same clothes twice and compulsively rinsed his hands in medical alcohol.

But it was in the area of nutrition that he took the greatest precautions to avoid contamination. **For foreign trips, a chemist-engineer in the securitate's Fifth Directorate was provided with a mobile laboratory and tasked with analysing and testing every morsel destined for the dictator's stomach.** All meals were specially prepared by one of the Ceausescus' entourage and transported to the couple's rooms in a sealed trolley with a lock whose combination was changed daily and known only to a valet.

Ceausescu was famously adept at avoiding meals that had not been screened; he shovelled everything served to him at formal banquets straight onto the floor, and kicked it has far away from him as possible.

His fellow Balkan dictator, the bon viveur Tito of Yugoslavia, took a famously dim view of Ceausescu lunching on his own simple vegetable juice, which he sucked through a straw.

COLIVA

Serves 6

*A cake traditionally only made and eaten at
funerals and memorial gatherings. The pot, Scotch
or hulled variety of barley used in it is rich in fibre.*

500g/ 1lb 10oz barley

300g/ 10oz granulated sugar

300g/ 10oz walnuts

3 tsp of vanilla essence

rind of a lemon

splash of rum

**For decoration with pious motifs any
combination of dried fruits, cocoa
powder, grated coconut and icing
sugar can be used**

Rinse the barley well in cold water.

Bring the washed barley to the boil in 3
times the quantity of water to barley, and
add a pinch of salt. Turn the heat down as
low as possible, and continue cooking for as
much as an hour and half. Remove any scum
from the surface of the water.

Only remove the pan from the heat when
all the water has either evaporated or been
absorbed and the barley grains have opened.
Test by squashing one between your fingers.

When cooked, add the sugar and mix well
for 4-5 minutes, so that nothing sticks to the
bottom of the pan. Add a splash of rum, the
walnuts and the lemon rind.

Decorate according to taste.

سماك التنور

تنور سمك

SADDAM HUSSEIN

1937 – 2006

Of humble stock and illiterate until the age of ten, Saddam Hussein grew up stealing eggs and chickens to support his family. He joined the military and became a leading light in Iraq's national socialist Ba'ath party. Rising to supreme power after the 1968 coup, he managed to consolidate his rule with the help of large oil revenues.

He lived with his wife, Sajida, for over forty years but had numerous mistresses and surrounded himself with an all-woman bodyguard posse. As his power grew so too did his family's extravagant lifestyle. Sajida enjoyed million-dollar shopping sprees to New York and London while their son, Uday, led a playboy existence collecting expensive cars and holding debauched parties.

The 'Great Uncle's' atrocious regime saw the use of chemical weapons against the Kurds in the north, the draining of marshland and annihilation of Shi'ite villages to the south and the waging of an 8-year-long war against Iran. Finally, his invasion of Kuwait in 1990 attracted the wrath of the US. He was defeated and Iraq subjected to over a decade of harsh sanctions. In 2003, the tendentious claim that he was hiding weapons of mass destruction provided President George W Bush and a coalition of the willing, including the UK, with the excuse needed to finish the job begun in 1990. Toppled and imprisoned by US forces, Saddam was executed in 2006 by an interim Iraqi government.

For all his infamously lavish lifestyle, Saddam was not a *gourmand*, like his younger son, Qusay, saying **'If we are satisfied only by food, we become worms or poultry'**. Maintaining his strong-man image involved looking super-fit and trim, with a little help from a skilful tailor and a strict swimming regime. Always careful about portion sizes, he tended to pick at his food, frequently leaving half of whatever was on his plate. He was fastidiously obsessed with cleanliness, ordering all utensils be thoroughly cleaned and he suggested that it would be better to bathe twice a day, especially if female, as **'It's not appropriate for someone to attend a gathering or to be with his children while his body odour trails behind him emitting sweet stinky smell mixed with perspiration'**.

Whatever was on his plate was always farm-fresh, flown to his palaces twice a week – sides of lamb and beef with the fat

trimmed off, fresh shrimps, live lobsters and his favourite olives from the Golan Heights – and all was thoroughly pre-checked for radiation or poison by his nuclear scientists. Kitchen staff at all twenty palaces simultaneously prepared three meals a day for him, for security reasons. **Poisoning was a constant and growing fear but he nonetheless had his oldest son, Uday, beaten up and hurled into jail for clubbing one of his food tasters to death.** On foreign trips, he took his own cooks. A long-lasting friendship with Fidel Castro was struck up in 1979 and Saddam was supplied regularly with cigars from Cuba from then on.

Particularly partial to fish and seafood, lean meat, fruit and vegetables, he was also fond of traditional Bedouin dishes. While a glass of Mateus Rosé might accompany his main meals, camel milk with bread and honey was his usual breakfast. He was partial to the odd glass of Old Parr whisky as well. His efforts to keep on top of his weight were often thwarted by his penchant for Quality Street sweets which many guests recall being offered.

The owner of a fish restaurant in Baghdad's Abu Nawaas Street recalls that Saddam's bodyguards would collect his order of fish twice a week. Iraq's national dish, *Masgouf*, or grilled carp, was always his favourite. Indeed Jacques Chirac, the former President of France, was greatly impressed with Masgouf having shared the fish with Saddam on a number of occasions. It was reported that Chirac had developed such a taste for Masgouf that Saddam had to arrange for one and a half tonnes of it be flown over to Chirac as a gift.

One of Saddam's former chefs has described how, on occasion, he would rouse his kitchen staff at '5 or 6 in the morning to grill some fish he'd just caught.' There were even times when Saddam appeared in the kitchen to lend a hand with the cooking: 'he used to say it made him relax.' Saddam's former Indian chef has happily recalled him also enjoying rasam lentil soup and chicken

biryani, while asking him to go easy on the salt and spices.

Once, as he chewed olives he told his former chief of intelligence he was spitting out the stones in **'the way I will one day spit out the Israelis from their land'.**

In those weeks he spent hiding out in a two-room shack in the countryside, evading capture in 2003, Saddam seems to have subsisted on simpler fare: on his capture eggs, honey and pistachio nuts were some of the items found in the fridge with a half-eaten tomato salad and nearly empty box of Bounty bars on a table nearby.

SAMAK MASGOUF

Serves 4 to 6

Dozens of restaurants line the Tigris in Baghdad with fish in tanks so that customers can choose their Carp to eat.

2 carp (trout, mullet or other large freshwater fish can be substituted)

3 tbsp olive oil

2 tbsp rock salt

1 tbsp tamarind paste

1 tsp turmeric

Black pepper

Tomato Salsa

500g/1lb tomatoes

2 onions

Salt, black pepper or spices of your choice

Cut the fish lengthwise, from their back without removing the skin. Gut, clean and wash thoroughly.

Brush the fish with the tamarind paste, turmeric and olive oil.

Start a wood fire, making sure that it has continual flames in order to achieve the smoky *masgouf* flavour.

Push two skewers longitudinally between the skin and the flesh on both sides of the fish.

Plant the skewers in the ground about 50cm from the fire, downwind so the fish is licked by flames and cook gently for 3 to 4 hours.

Heat oil in a frying pan. Chop onions very thin and add them to the pan. Cut tomatoes into small pieces and add them to the onion. Add salt and black pepper to the mix. Cook for 10 minutes or until you have a thick sauce mixture in the frying pan.

Remove the fish once it's well cooked. Put it on a tray or plate. Brush the sauce on its inside.

Iraqi pickles are a good accompaniment with some freshly baked crispy flatbread.

MUAMMAR GADDAFI

1942 – 2011

Born in a tent near Sirte, Gaddafi hailed from a humble, nomadic family. After a stint of military training in Beaconsfield, UK he launched a bloodless coup d'état back in Libya in 1969.

He had two wives, numerous mistresses, a daughter and a number of infamous sons including the footballer al-Saadi who tested positive for anabolic steroids while playing for Perugia. Another hapless son, Hannibal, was arrested for assaulting a chambermaid in Switzerland thus triggering a stream of retaliatory actions by Gaddafi – Swiss nationals were arrested, diplomats expelled – ultimately leading Gaddafi to moot the idea of abolishing Switzerland. Swiftly ejecting all Italians from the country, he nationalised its oil industry.

His famous Green Book rejected both capitalism and communism, proposing instead a 'Third Universal Theory' which bears similarities to the Yugoslav Third Way of self-management under Tito. He was implicated in various nefarious activities overseas, including shipping arms to the IRA, the shooting of PC Yvonne Fletcher in London and the explosion of a Pan Am flight over Lockerbie in 1998.

He avoided at least a dozen attempts on his life throughout his rule before his gruesome murder in the Libyan uprising of 2011.

Self-proclaimed 'Dean of Arab Rulers, the King of Kings of Africa and Imam of Muslims', Gaddafi liked to be thought of as 'Brother Leader' by his people while those closest to him referred to him as 'Papa' and those who were not so fond of him simply called him 'Mad Dog'.

A vain man, he surrounded himself with glamorous female bodyguards wearing lipstick and high heels and loyal nurses whose job it was to ensure that he was fit, healthy and eternally youthful. His fear of catching diseases bordered on obsessive. As the ravages of age caught up with him he sought hair implants and plastic surgery to remain alluring. Perhaps Gaddafi's superior dental work proved a bigger draw than his wealth and power

for the more than one hundred women who responded to his Italian newspaper advertisement for attractive women under the age of 35. *Al Zaht al Akhdar* newspaper gushed on the subject: **'His teeth are naturally immune to stain so that when he releases a full-blown smile, the naturally white teeth discharge a radiation pregnant with sweet joy and real happiness for those lucky ones who are fortunate enough to be around him'.**

The camel milk Gaddafi liked to drink may have enhanced the brilliant whiteness of his smile but it seems to have played havoc with his digestion. Whether he suffered from uncontrollable flatulence or whether, on the other hand, he was able to exploit this affliction to emphasize whatever point he was engaged in making, as demonstrated in an interview with John Simpson, is debatable. Certainly, on a visit to his tent in 2004, Tony Blair was advised not to accept a glass of camel milk, lest he be similarly afflicted.

Hospitable himself, Gaddafi was not so comfortable accepting others' hospitality. On a visit to Belgrade in 1961 **he insisted on pitching his tent directly in front of his hotel,** along with his camels that would graze outside and provide him with the odd glass of milk. He was outraged when Washington refused him permission to do the same in New York's Central Park twenty years later.

In accordance with Islam and the tenets of his Green Book Gaddafi didn't drink alcohol, banning its consumption in Libya. He wasn't fond of Pepsi or Coca-Cola either, announcing in Conakry, Guinea in 2007 that 'Whenever I ask about Pepsi-Cola or Coca-Cola, people immediately say it is an American or European drink. This is not true. The kola is African. They have taken the cheap raw material from us. They produced it, they made it into a drink, and they sell it to us for a high price. Why are Pepsi-Cola and Coca-Cola expensive? Because they have taken our kola, produced it, and sold it back to us. We should produce it ourselves and sell it to them.'

Despite banishing Italians from Libya early on in his reign, Gaddafi was a close friend of Silvio Berlusconi and retained a fondness for Italian food, including pastries and pasta dishes, in particular macaroni. Libyan macaroni, Mbekbka, has a rather ingenious method of cooking the pasta with the sauce to retain the pasta flavour, rather than boiling in water and then mixing with sauce. However, he enjoyed simple Libyan food just as much as any Italian dish and his native couscous with camel meat was a particular favourite.

CAMEL MEAT & COUSCOUS

Serves 6

Camel meat can be bought online in the UK, generally imported from Australia, and needs slow cooking. Lamb or beef make good substitutes. The hump is the most prized cut and can be boiled or roasted. A couscoussier is the proper cooking vessel for this dish; it comprises an upper pot, a kiskas, with tiny holes in the bottom of it which sits on the lower pot, a gdrah in which the meat and vegetables stew, the marga, slowly simmers. A colander placed on top of a stock pot is a useful alternative.

3 tbsp olive oil

2 medium onions, finely chopped

I can of chickpeas

2 tbsp of tomato paste

Salt and pepper

2 tsp of cinnamon

II/ 2pt of water

Rose water

1kg/2lb 4oz camel meat diced

2 cinnamon sticks

3 cardamom pods

2 bay leaves

2 tsp cayenne pepper

500g/ 1lb couscous – traditional, not instant

(Some versions add prunes to deliver a sweeter texture to the meat.)

Heat I tbsp of olive oil in pan. Add and cook half the onions until golden.

Stir in the chickpeas and I tbsp of tomato paste, season with salt, pepper and I tsp of cinnamon then add 150ml of the water.

Reduce the heat and cook slowly for 55 minutes, adding water if it is drying out in that time. Sprinkle with rose water and dust with cinnamon. Cover, remove from heat and set aside.

Heat 2 tablespoons of oil and cook the remaining onions slowly for 10 to 15 minutes until golden.

Add the camel meat, cinnamon sticks, cardamom and bay leaves. Stir to combine and cook on low heat until meat has browned and juices have evaporated. Add the remaining tomato paste and cayenne pepper and stir to coat the camel meat. Add 800ml of water and bring to a low boil.

In a medium-sized bowl, stir together the couscous, I tsp of salt, a sprinkle of rose water and the remaining 50ml of water.

Place the top portion of the couscoussier, or colander, over the lower pan with the meat mixture in it and add the couscous mixture to the top portion. Slowly steam for 90 minutes.

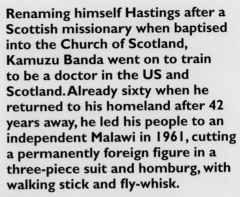

HASTINGS KAMUZU BANDA

1898 – 1997

Renaming himself Hastings after a Scottish missionary when baptised into the Church of Scotland, Kamuzu Banda went on to train to be a doctor in the US and Scotland. Already sixty when he returned to his homeland after 42 years away, he led his people to an independent Malawi in 1961, cutting a permanently foreign figure in a three-piece suit and homburg, with walking stick and fly-whisk.

Although soundly progressive on women's rights and education, he required a large posse of women dancers wearing cloth with his portrait on, to entertain him wherever he went. Under his puritanical rule, Malawi was one of the last countries to have televisions in the nineties. Kissing was banned in public and edited from films. Books were censored and private mail read. Phone calls were tapped and lines cut dead. He outlawed hippies and mini-skirts, and visitors seeking visas were informed 'female passengers will not be permitted to enter the country if wearing short dresses or trouser suits, except in transit or at lake holiday resorts or national parks. Skirts and dresses must cover the knees to conform with government regulations. The entry of hippies and men with long hair and flared trousers is forbidden'.

He turned Malawi into a single party republic, declaring himself President for Life and introduced a network of secret agents – his 'Young Pioneers' who effectively dealt with any opponents at home and abroad, ensuring that they became, in his words, 'food for crocodiles.' Ousted in 1994, he died in exile in South Africa.

A popular belief that Banda the young medical student had died in the US, to be replaced by a foreign impostor – a Richard Armstrong – was in large part sustained by the simple fact that Banda was unable to speak Chichewa and never liked or ate the national dish, *nsima*, a thick, starchy porridge made from maize that accompanies almost every Malawian meal. It is rolled into a ball and dipped into sauce. Instead of *nsima* Banda – or Armstrong – ate rice, despite encouraging the farmers of Malawi to grow maize.

We have, however, his Official Hostess' word for it that Banda thoroughly relished other Malawian specialities. Cecilia Tamanda Kadzamira, who was never his wife but became known as the Mama of the nation, has recalled that *nkhwani wo tendera*,

pumpkin leaves with peanut powder; *masamba*, greens with tomatoes; *nkwanya*, bean leaves; *mfutso*, dried leafy vegetables and the small *matemba* fish found in Lake Malawi, were some of his favourites. **Banda was also very partial to mopane worms; he apparently liked them best when 'simply dried and then eaten as a snack like crisps,'** and was in the habit of keeping a few of them in his pockets to dole out to any children he encountered on his tours of inspection around the country. The mopane worm is the large caterpillar of the emperor moth and can be eaten dry, crunchy like potato chips or cooked with sauce.

Ms Kadzamira, who effectively ruled the country during Banda's waning last years as president, recalled him telling her a revealing story about his impoverished childhood

in what was then British-ruled Nyasaland.
While still only a boy, he was forced to
go out hunting for food to help feed his
multiple siblings. One day, he happened
across a leopard halfway through eating an
antelope it had killed. Banda approached
the leopard on all fours, fixed it with an
unblinking stare and, finally, watched it slink
off, defeated, leaving the rest of its dinner
unattended. Half an antelope added up to a
useful family forage.

Banda's western medical training made him
particularly aware of the importance of a
healthy diet. **An early adopter of free-
range meat, especially chicken and
beef, he also regularly ate greens.** He
was teetotal, a non-smoker and a believer in
regular non-impact exercise such as walking.

MOPANI WORMS

Serves 2

Mopani (or mopane) worms contain 3 times the amount of protein as beef but are more environmentally friendly as the worms obviously eat less than a cow.

Pluck the worms as they cling, feeding on the leaves of the mopane trees. These worms can be as long as 6" and around 3/4" thick.

The worms will excrete a brown liquid when making contact with human flesh.

Squeeze out the green, slimy entrails of the worm. Leave out in the hot sun for a few days to dry out.

Once they have dried out they can be eaten straight away or they can be cooked in a spicy or peanut butter sauce.

Nkhwani Wo Tendera
Pumpkin Leaves in Peanut Powder Stew

Almost any green vegetable can be used instead of pumpkin leaves – kale, spinach, sweet potato leaves work well.

400g / 1lb green leaves, destalked

½ tsp salt

4 medium tomatoes, chopped

4 tbsp peanuts, ground to a fine powder using grinder or pestle and mortar

2 small onions, chopped

Put the greens into enough boiling water to just cover them and cook over a medium heat for about 10 mins until they are soft, adding more water if necessary, to keep them from sticking to the pan.

After a minute or so, place the tomatoes, onions and peanut powder on top of the greens, do not stir.

Place a lid over the pot and stir, then simmer for another 30 mins or so until the powder smells and tastes cooked.

Serve with dried mopani worms.

JEAN BEDEL BOKASSA

1921 – 1996

Jean Bedel Bokassa joined French Equatorial Guinea's colonial army and distinguished himself fighting for France in Indochina. His cousin, the president, appointed him head of newly independent Central African Republic's armed forces but Bokassa repaid the favour by leading a coup to oust his relative in 1966, before embarking on a 13-year reign that earned him a reputation as Africa's gaudiest dictator.

His era featured extravagant spending on the paraphernalia of a 19th century European-style monarchy, but also the slaughter of 100 schoolchildren who protested against an obligation to buy overpriced uniforms from a company owned by one of Bokassa's wives. Credible rumours of cannibalism surrounded the man President Valéry Giscard d'Estaing referred to as his 'friend and family member'. It was said that if Bokassa didn't eat his enemies, he fed them to the crocodiles in his private zoo.

In 1975, in a ceremony inspired by Napoleon's coronation, Bokassa crowned himself Emperor of a Central African Empire. He was removed from power by a French-backed coup in 1979, but comfortably exiled to Paris. Although sentenced to death in absentia, he chose to return to his homeland in 1987 for a retrial in which his sentence was commuted to life imprisonment. He died a free man in Bangui, of a heart attack, in 1996.

One reason why the French had decided that enough of their man, Jean Bedel Bokassa, was more than enough by 1979 was a passing remark he made at the banquet accompanying a coronation ceremony he had modelled as closely as possible on that of Napoleon, complete with an antique coach, gilded throne shaped like an eagle, fur-lined robes, Belgian thoroughbred horses, sixty Mercedes, champagne and caviar. **'You never noticed, but you ate human flesh,'** Bokassa had observed to France's Minister for Development.

Paris Match had then run with the ball by printing photographs of palace fridges filled with corpses, and the French forces involved in Bokassa's 1979 overthrow did indeed discover two refrigerated corpses at his Villa Kolongo — one, that of a former maths teacher.

In 1987, when Bokassa returned to Bangui from exile to stand trial, his former cook, Philippe Linguissa, claimed that his master had once asked him to prepare a feast from one of the corpses he would find in the walk-in fridge in the kitchen. **'Bokassa gave me a razor and told me to clean it and stuff it with rice,'** Linguissa informed the courtroom, explaining that he'd gone on to douse it in gin and flambé it. He also recalled Bokassa sitting down to eat it the following morning, removing his shirt for maximum comfort. However, his evidence was thrown out when he proved incapable of remembering even the gender of the corpse.

The cannibalism charge could not be made to stick. Bokassa claimed that the photos Paris-Match had published had not shown his refrigerator; **'what they showed was the freezer from the morgue, which you can go and see for yourself. It's still there,' he insisted. How could a many times decorated former French soldier such as himself, he asked one journalist, be a cannibal?**

But a well-researched and lengthy Vanity Fair article that was published at the time of the trial pointed out that Bokassa belonged to the M'baka tribe, one nationally renowned for its custom of eating human flesh in the belief that it would make its members braver, stronger, more handsome and more intelligent.

It is hard to imagine a less cannibal diet than that of most Central African Republicans.

SPINACH STEW & FU-FU

Serves 4-6

Fufu is a stiff porridge, usually made with cassava which women boil every day and then pound in a pestle and mortar. Cornmeal can be substituted for cassava.

Fufu

260g/ 10oz of white cornmeal

240ml/ 8fl.oz milk

240ml/ 8fl.oz water

Spinach Stew

2 small onions, chopped

2tbsp oil

2 tomatoes, peeled and sliced

1 green bell pepper, chopped

900g/ 2lb fresh spinach, chopped or about 1kg/ 2lb 2oz of frozen spinach

1tsp salt

2 red chili peppers, sliced, or ½ tsp of cayenne pepper

4tbsp smooth peanut butter

Fufu

Heat a cup of water in a medium saucepan.

Pour milk into a bowl and add the cornmeal slowly, stirring briskly to make a smooth paste.

Add this mix to the boiling water, stirring constantly and cook for 4-5 minutes, adding any leftover cornmeal. Remove from heat when the mixture begins to pull away from the sides of the pan and stick together.

Put fufu in a greased bowl and, with damp hands, shape it into a smooth ball, turning it in the bowl to smooth it.

Serve immediately.

Spinach Stew

Fry the onions in a heavy-bottomed casserole pan until soft and golden. Add the sliced tomatoes and green pepper and cook for approximately 1 minute.

Add spinach, salt and hot red pepper. Cover, reduce heat and simmer for 5 minutes

Thin the peanut butter with a few tbsps of warm water to make a smooth paste. Add to stew

Cook for another 10-15 minutes, stirring frequently and taking care not to let the stew burn. Add water to stop it sticking to pan.

Serve with fufu or rice.

DICTATORS' DINNERS

IDI AMIN

1925 – 2003

Idi Amin served as a cook in a British colonial regiment, before rising through the ranks to major general in the post-independence Ugandan army and seizing power in a military coup in 1971.

During eight years of atrocious and manic misrule he killed up to half a million of his people, expelled some 60,000 Ugandan Asians and declared himself Field Marshal, Lord of all Beasts of the Earth and Fishes of the Sea, and even a CBE – Conqueror of the British Empire – when Britain broke off diplomatic relations with him. In time Harold Wilson would describe him as 'mentally unbalanced' whilst Mr Kaunda thought he was a 'madman and buffoon'. Others believed that he suffered from syphilis which was leading to brain damage. Julius Nyerere described him as 'a murderer, a liar and a savage'.

The Anglican Bishop of Kampala was assassinated in a bogus car crash and many ministers were thrown to the crocodiles in Lake Victoria under his orders. War with Tanzania triggered his downfall and flight into exile, first to Libya and finally to Saudi Arabia for 24 years where he died from kidney failure.

Idi Amin loved most things British – Church's shoes, cravats, well-tailored suits, silver cutlery and afternoon tea. One journalist has recalled enjoying cucumber sandwiches, scones and cake with Amin, as compensation for being accidentally punched by one of his bodyguards. Once, hearing that Britain was facing tough economic times, Amin consoled Queen Elizabeth II: 'I'm sending a cargo ship of bananas to thank you for the good days of the colonial administration.' **He was particularly captivated by Britain's monarch, inviting her to Uganda to meet a 'real man' and sent her love letters.** To celebrate the silver anniversary of her coronation he suggested she send

him her '25 year old knickers.' Whether this was venereal mad delusion or an obsessive crush is unclear but it appears his attentions were unappreciated and the Queen unmoved by his magnetism and the deep seductive timbre of his voice. This may have contributed to his later disillusionment with the English and his offer to help the Scottish break away and **proclaim himself 'the Last King of Scotland'.**

Rumours of cannibalism swirled about him. It was said that on taking power he had had all his military rivals rounded up and decapitated before perching on a pile of their heads and taking bites out of their faces. This was perfectly, it was said, in accordance with a belief held by Amin's

Kakwa tribe that if enemy flesh was eaten, the enemy's spirit couldn't return to haunt the killer. Asked point-blank once if he was a cannibal, Amin replied, **'I don't like human flesh – it's too salty for me.'**

Cannibalism aside, one of Amin's dozens of children has recalled a first characteristically cruel encounter with his father at the age of four. Sweating over a plate of chicken, Amin invited him to taste the food, without warning him it was deluged in the hottest red chilli sauce. While the little boy screamed in shock and pain, Amin roared with laughter.

A particularly noteworthy state banquet hosted by Idi Amin included bee larvae, green bush crickets, cicadas, flying ants and locusts. Fried grasshoppers and crickets are a particular treat in Uganda. Fried grasshoppers can be bought from street vendors or their torsos bought alive from the market. In order to cook them they need to be washed thoroughly and fried with a little onion and garlic with salt and pepper to taste.

He was a formidable man of 6ft 4 inches, a former heavyweight boxing champion

so that during his sedentary life in exile in Saudi Arabia his girth increased considerably despite his daily routine of a swim and massage in local 5 star hotels. His love of pizza, meat and Kentucky Fried Chicken contributed to his weight gain along with frequent jaunts to fast food restaurants with his family to feast on burgers followed by afternoon tea in nearby hotels. He spent lazy days fishing in the Red Sea, reciting the Quran, watching satellite television and playing the accordion.

A voracious appetite for oranges – as many as 40 a day, it is said – on account of their claim to be 'Nature's Viagra', earned him the nickname Mr Jaffa. His favourite food was Roast Goat, Cassava and millet bread and he could often be found at Jeddah airport expectantly waiting for cassava and millet flour sent from his relatives in Uganda.

MILLET BREAD & LUWOMBO

Serves 4

Kalo is commonly made using millet and cassava flour. This recipe uses cassava and sorghum flour, but any combination of flours can be used. It is usually rolled into a ball with the hand and dipped into sauce or stew.

Kalo (Millet Bread)

750ml/1 ½ pts water
150g/5oz cassava flour
150g/5oz sorghum flour

Luwombo

1kg / 2lb goat meat, chopped into small bite-size chunks
110g/4oz of finely ground peanuts
2 onions, finely chopped
1 chicken stock cube
125g/4 ½oz of mushrooms, sliced
Salt and pepper
Banana leaves

Kalo (Millet Bread)

Boil the water in a pan.

Add the flour and stir briskly over a medium heat, smoothing the lumps of flour.

With time, it will begin to form one large ball. When its consistency is sticky rather than runny and it can hold its shape, it's ready.

Luwombo

Sauté the goat meat in a lightly oiled pan until browned. Set aside.

Heat 1 tbsp of oil in a pan, add the onions and cook for two minutes Add the tomatoes, stock cube, salt and pepper, ground peanuts, mushrooms and some water if necessary, to make a smooth sauce.

Simmer for 8 to 10 minutes. Add the meat to the mixture.

Cut the banana leaves into 10-inch wide rectangles and remove the middle ribs. Hold each leaf above a flame for a few seconds to soften them, then rinse in water.

Place a portion of the meat mixture in the middle of the leaf and fold the leaf to form a little parcel. Tie with string and repeat the procedure with the rest of the mixture.

Place a rack in the bottom of a large pot and add water.

Place the banana leaf parcels on the rack and cover the pot with a lid. Steam for at least 2 hours.

Serve the parcels with mashed cassava.

MOBUTU SESE SEKO

1930 – 1997

The lowly born son of a cook, Mobutu was nurtured and taught French by a white woman, and had joined the military when Congo achieved independence from Belgium in 1960. He was soon Chief of Staff and the recipient of significant US and Belgian support against the democratically elected but Left-leaning Patrice Lumumba. A couple of military coups later, by 1965, he had emerged on top, to begin his 32-year period of rule over a wildly dysfunctional kleptocracy which he renamed Zaire.

Instantly recognisable in his leopard skin pill-box hat and Buddy Holly specs carrying an eagle-headed wooden sceptre, he embarked on a campaign of 'Africanisation' and by the end of his rule had embezzled up to 15 billion dollars of the country's mineral wealth. Internationally he is probably best remembered for 'The Rumble in the Jungle', a fight between George Foreman and Muhammad Ali which drew huge publicity to Zaire.

His eviction from the country by rebels in 1997 brought to an end a regime which saw a cult of personality so extreme that at the beginning of each newscast Mobutu descending from the clouds in the heavens was broadcast to the nation. He died in Morocco of prostate cancer three months later.

An under-privileged childhood, in which he depended for food and clothing on relatives, rather than his own father who had disappeared, may explain why Mobutu's appetite for everything – fine food and drink, cars, palaces and suits – was so excessive and insatiable.

On achieving power, his lifestyle can only be described as imperial, especially once he'd built his 100 million dollar Versailles in the Jungle, his Gbadolite Palace, which boasted a landing strip long enough to accommodate not just standard-sized aeroplanes ferrying fresh seafood, meat, flowers and patisserie from Europe, but also Concorde. Visitors spoke of the 'salon' being stocked with a large selection of cognacs and spirits whilst others remember dining on roast quail, salmon and paté.

Up at half past six every morning, he was being worked on by a team of Chinese masseurs by seven. An hour later, breakfasting on his terrace, he would be feeding a few crumbs to the peacocks which patrolled the formal gardens while perusing the foreign press. In his study by nine, it was time to start work but also to crack open a first bottle of his favourite tipple, **Laurent Perrier pink champagne.** Mussels flown straight in from Zeebrugge for one of his favourite lunches, *moules frites*, would be perfectly accompanied by a vintage wine.

With its antique-filled rooms and marble floors, Gbadolite was the perfect venue for his daughter's wedding. Doubtless wilting in that swampy equatorial climate, 2,500 guests were served fresh lobster, salmon and caviar, and a thousand bottles of Grand Cru wines from Mobutu's own wine-cellar. The wedding cake was a four-metre square confection of meringue and whipped cream, prepared by a chef in Paris that very morning and flown over on its own chilled chartered flight, at a cost of roughly $65,000. All of which was somewhat at odds with 'Mobutuism' where African traditions were to be adhered to including cuisine, dress, dance and culture. European suits and ties were forbidden and in their place 'Abacosts' (abbreviation of French for 'à bas le costume' – 'down with the suit') could be worn with a cravat. Mobutu changed his name to Mobutu Sese Seko which has the rather catchy translation of **'the all-conquering warrior who, because of his endurance and inflexible will to win, will go from conquest to conquest leaving fire in his wake'**.

Mobutu's paranoia rendered life as dangerous for the Congolese as Stalin's paranoia had for the Russians. For example, news of four or five heads of state enterprises gathered together for dinner was cause for alarm and suspicion. Once, when Mobutu himself was a guest at dinner but suddenly felt too poorly to stay, he had a waitress report back on every word uttered by the other guests about his failing health. One by one, each of them lost their jobs.

In his declining years, Mobutu took up yoga and became a vegetarian as part of a quest to lose weight.

MOULES MARINIÈRE

Serves 4

4½lb fresh mussels in their shells, beards removed

2 medium onions, chopped

2 cloves of garlic, crushed

A handful of parsley stalks

Salt and freshly ground black pepper

300ml / ½ pint of dry white wine

3 tbsp of chopped fresh parsley

4 tbsp of single cream

Clean the mussels by scrubbing them well under running water, removing any beards, barnacles and grit. Tap any that are slightly open and, if they fail to close, discard them together with any whose shells are cracked. Rinse again under running water.

Heat a pan large enough to easily hold all the mussels. Add onion and garlic and fry in a little butter until softened.

Add the mussels and wine and bring to the boil. Cover tightly with a lid and then reduce the heat to a simmer for 10 minutes, until the onion is soft.

Remove the lid, bring back to the boil and add the mussels. Replace the lid and cook over a high heat for about 5 minutes, shaking the pan from time to time, until all the mussels are open. Add the chopped parsley and cream.

MENGISTU HAILE MARIAM

b. 1937

With Soviet backing and Communist East Germany for inspiration, Mengistu – nicknamed the 'Red Negus' – ousted Ethiopia's popular old Emperor Haile Selassie in 1974 (rumours suggesting Mengistu suffocated Selassie with a pillow persist) and set about impoverishing and terrorising his country.

Brutal programmes of 'resettlement' and 'villagisation' in the 1970s – reminiscent of Stalin's deportations and collectivisation campaign in the 1930s – were followed by the famines of the 1980s in his new-look People's Democratic Republic of Ethiopia. Human Rights Watch rated Mengistu's Red Terror 'one of the most systematic uses of mass murder by a state ever witnessed in Africa', costing around half a million lives. 'Kebeles' (neighbourhood vigilantes) executed students, teachers and intellectuals. Corpses of children were piled up in the street with families having to pay a ransom for the bullet used to retrieve their bodies.

Wars with neighbouring countries combined with deserted farms and drought led to the famine of 1983-5 which hit eight million Ethiopians and left a further million dead despite a huge international humanitarian effort which included $1 billion relief .Overthrown in 1991, Mengistu fled to Zimbabwe, to be welcomed by Robert Mugabe and given a home in Harare. In 2006, he was tried in absentia back in Addis Ababa, and found guilty of genocide.

A famine so appalling that BBC footage of skeletal babies and Michael Buerk dubbing it **'the closest thing to hell on Earth'** galvanised Bob Geldof into mounting his Band Aid campaign and the world's attention was caught, just as Mengistu was revving up to a grand celebration of the tenth anniversary of his revolution. Disgusted UN aid workers noted that many of Ethiopia's aeroplanes were being used to fly in whisky for the regime's birthday shindig rather than grain for the starving masses.

Johnny Walker Black Label was reportedly Mengistu's tipple of choice, rather than Ethiopia's native honey-based wine, *tej* which had been his alcoholic father's favourite. Later, at the start of his Zimbabwean exile, Mengistu would haunt Harare's downtown bars, often so drunk that his bodyguards deserted him, complaining that he beat them up.

However, he remained staunchly loyal to his country's indigenous foods, the most famous of which is *injera*. A spongy, pleasantly sour,

pancake-like bread, Ethiopians use it both as a utensil to dip into various sauces and stews and as a tablecloth on which to place other foods, to be eaten in its turn, once everything else has been consumed. It is made from *teff*, each tiny grain of which contains more iron and seventeen times more calcium than either wheat or barley. Best of all in the eyes of western nutritionists who are beginning to wonder if its special properties might account for Ethiopians' freedom from diabetes and other common western afflictions, *teff* is gluten-free. There is even a growing suspicion that **teff**-rich injera might be responsible for the extraordinary stamina and endurance of Ethiopian athletes.

The sauces and stews that accompany injera are known as *wot* and are frequently very spicy. Mengistu's favourite *wot* is made of chickpeas and is called Shiro Wot. Like most other *wots* it owes much of its inimitably subtle flavour to a blend of spices known as Berbere, which can be made up at home or bought ready-mixed in many supermarkets.

SHIRO WOT & INGERA

Serves 2

Shiro powders vary in what powdered legumes they include (dried peas, lentils, broad beans, chickpeas). When making the *Shiro Wot* stew, the powder is reconstituted with water and in Ethiopia cooks listen for a 'tuk tuk' sound which tells them it has reached the right consistency. *Berbere* spice is a mixture of spices toasted and ground up and can include any or all of the following spices – cumin seeds, fenugreek seeds, black peppercorns, whole allspice, cloves, sweet paprika, hot paprika, ground cardamom, ground ginger, salt flakes, coriander, turmeric and cinnamon.

Shiro Wot (Stew)

75g/ 3oz shiro powder

1 small onion, finely chopped

2 cloves of garlic, finely chopped

60ml/ 2fl.oz olive oil

1tsp Berbere spice

600ml/1 pt water

salt to taste

Ingera
Makes 4-6, You will need to begin this recipe two days ahead.

200g/7oz teff flour,(can be a mixture of sorghum and teff) or plain flour

250ml/8fl.oz water

½ tsp baking powder

Pinch of salt

Coconut oil for pan

Shiro Wot (Stew)

In a medium pan sauté the onion and garlic in olive oil for 3 to 4 minutes. Add the Berbere spice and two tbsp of water, and simmer for about 5 minutes, stirring occasionally.

Add the remaining water to the pan and carefully whisk in the shiro powder, a tsp at a time, until completely combined.

Allow it to cook on a low heat for about 30 minutes, until it has a thick but smooth consistency. The key to a good Shiro Wot is letting it simmer slowly on a low heat until it is a creamy stew rather than runny liquid.

Add salt to taste and serve with *injera*.

Ingera

Put teff flour in large bowl. Add water and stir well. Cover with tea towel and allow to stand for 1-2 days until bubbles appear. Do not stir. The mixture should have the consistency of pancake batter.

Heat a pan on medium heat and lightly coat the pan with the coconut oil.

Stir a little salt into the batter and then stir in the baking powder. The batter will deflate as the mixture is stirred.

Pour enough batter into pan to coat the surface of the pan and cover with a lid. It is important to keep the moisture in the *injera* or it will crack. Cook for about 5-7 minutes when the top will start to bubble and dry out.

Remove from the pan with a spatula. Pile the *injera* on a plate with greaseproof paper separating them.

DICTATORS' DINNERS

FRANCISCO MACIAS NGUEMA

1920 – 1979

Born into Spain's only sub-Saharan African colony, Nguema was elected independent Equatorial Guinea's first president in 1968 and swiftly set about reversing the country's enviable educational and economic achievements.

All opposition was quashed and in 1970 Equatorial Guinea became a Single Party State. Ten of his original twelve cabinet members were killed and he established 'the Youth on the March with Macias', a group who terrorised the population through torture, executions and burning of villages. Between one and two thirds of the population fled 'the Dachau of Africa' or were killed during Macias' incumbency.

Uncertain of his intellectual credentials having three times failed his civil service exams, Nguema banned the word 'intellectual', along with newspapers and printing presses. The brain drain that ensued along with the migrant worker exodus led to the destruction of the economy. Agricultural output, in particular, cocoa plummeted. The situation was exacerbated when the director of the Central Bank was executed and Macias took the National Treasure and stored it in one of his palaces. As the economy failed he came up with a cunning ruse for money making. When a Soviet plane crashed into a mountain killing those on board in 1976, he refused to release the bodies until compensation of $5 million was paid for damage to the mountain.

In 1979, 'Africa's Pol Pot' was sentenced to death '101 times' by a Moroccan firing squad at Black Beach Prison, where Simon Mann was later held.

The son of a witch-doctor of Equatorial Guinea's largest ethnic group, the Fang, Nguema was steeped in his people's ancient rituals and beliefs. With his ban on western medicine causing a resurgence of ancient native remedies and witchcraft in the country, he also promoted a reversion to the pre-colonial habit of honouring one's ancestors by adorning village meeting places with human skulls. Rumours of his cannibalism abounded and he was said to be building up a personal collection of skulls in his refrigerator at home.

Many believe that Nguema's mounting paranoia, not to mention his isolation, his unpredictability, bizarre commandments and utter indifference to his people's suffering, were caused and then exacerbated by regular recourse to two mind-altering substances. **How else to explain his 1975 decision to have 150 of his opponents taken to Malabo stadium** **and killed by troops dressed as Santa Clauses, to the accompaniment of 'Those Were the Days' by Mary Hopkins?**

He was partial to *bhang*, a tea made from the leaves and buds of the female cannabis plant. Easily sourced because cannabis grows in abundance among Equatorial Guinea's

cassava plants and banana trees, it is commonly believed to enhance consumers' courage, imagination and inspiration. His pronouncement that he was **'God's Unique Miracle' and 'God created Equatorial Guinea thanks to Papa Macias Nguema'** could be attributed to drug induced grandiose ideas. He also made free with *iboga*, a root bark found uniquely in the rainforests of the region. Crushed almost to a powder, *iboga* is used in small amounts in the Fang's religious initiation ceremonies, but its hallucinogenic properties mean that when consumed in larger quantities people experience visions and closer connection to the afterlife and ancestors. It was doubtless while under the influence of these drugs that Nguema reportedly regularly sat down to dinner with imaginary guests.

Fish – real or imagined – would probably not have been on the menu since he had banned all fishing vessels from setting sail in an effort to stop more people fleeing his rule. Presumably there was no problem sourcing chicken because Nguema is on the record as having 'discarded chicken bones under the presidential table during dinner'. He may have washed down a traditional chicken in a peanut sauce dish with local palm wine or *malamba*, made from fermented sugarcane.

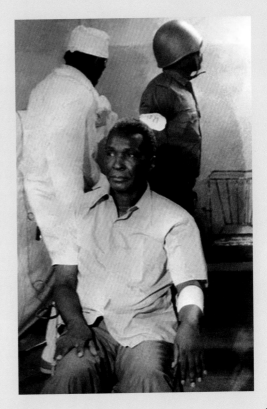

POLLO CON SALSA DE CACAHUETES

Chicken with Peanut Sauce
Serves 6

The cuisine of Equatorial Guinea combines indigenous tribal tradition with that of its former Spanish colonial cuisine. Cassava, plantains, yams, banana, leafy greens and locally hunted game and fish feature widely in the cuisine. Popular dishes include grilled fish with pumpkin seeds and guinea fowl paella.

2 1/4 pints water
1 medium chicken
2 tbsp tomato paste
2 cloves of garlic, chopped
1 white onion, chopped
2 stock cubes
250g/ 9oz peanut butter
1 tbsp lemon juice
Pinch of cayenne pepper
1 habanero chilli
Olive oil for frying

Joint the chicken into six portions.

Fry the onion and garlic in oil in a large pan over a medium heat until soft.

Pound the tomato paste and chilli together and add to the pan with the chicken. Stir well and continue to fry for a few minutes.

Add all remaining ingredients – lemon juice, cayenne pepper, peanut butter, stock cube, wáter and peanut butter. Turn up the heat and bring to boil. Turn down heat and simmer for 45 minutes covered on a low heat until the chicken is cooked.

Add salt and pepper to taste.

Serve with rice or boiled plantains.

KWAME NKRUMAH

1909 – 1972

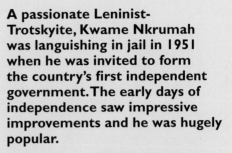

A passionate Leninist-Trotskyite, Kwame Nkrumah was languishing in jail in 1951 when he was invited to form the country's first independent government. The early days of independence saw impressive improvements and he was hugely popular.

Queues would form with expectant people hoping for marital advice, financial advice or even miracles from him. So it is no surprise that he slept little – he worked an 18 hour day – and ate meagre amounts. According to Erica Powell his personal secretary and confidante, he was a lonely figure who found it hard to trust others. However, by 1958 he was over-taxing Ghana's cocoa farmers to pay for lavish schemes including an expensive hydro-electric dam crossing the Volta and was fast making enemies. By 1964 he had declared himself president for life, banned strikes and granted himself powers to arrest and detain opponents; 'even a system based on a democratic constitution may need backing up in the period following independence by emergency measures of a totalitarian kind', was how he explained himself.

Prisoners were held without trial and he increasingly withdrew to Christiansborg Castle, surrounding himself with sycophants and becoming divorced from the politics and economy of Ghana. Overthrown by a military coup in 1965, Nkrumah never regained power or returned to Ghana and died of cancer in Romania. In 1978 his widow accepted an award in New York from the UN for his fight against apartheid and in 2000 he was voted Africa's Man of the Millennium by BBC World Service listeners.

Nkrumah's life was consumed by politics – to the exclusion of everything else. Sports, hobbies, family life and even his nutrition all took a backseat. **He postponed the thought of marriage until 1957 when he married an Egyptian named Fathia whom he gave the flattering nickname 'rabbit' because she liked to have a green salad accompanying each meal.** Although she taught their chef some Egyptian dishes, and she came to love the Ghanaian food *kenkey,* a steamed dough ball made from fermented maize as well as Kontomire (cocoyam leaf stew) made with smoked fish; the couple never learned to speak each other's languages and he refused to have Fathia and their 3 children join him in exile.

Even from an early age, Nkrumah showed little interest in food, recalling in his autobiography how this had worried his parents so much that his mother began popping baked plantain under his pillow in the hope he might fancy a midnight snack. Later, as a poor student in London, he haunted the cheaper cafés of Camden, talking politics with like-minded Africans for hours, only very occasionally splashing out on a bun with his single cup of tea.

Hard at work with an organisation devoted to ending colonial rule in West Africa he would do the rounds of the hotel dustbins in Gray's Inn Road, foraging for fish heads to make traditional Ghanaian stews. Much later on, official visitors to Ghana would be astonished to observe President Nkrumah at table, **'delving with a serving**

**spoon in the bowl to locate a fish-
head which he would then place
on their plate as a great delicacy'.**

While still in prison, Nkrumah had fasted
two days a week, for two reasons. Firstly, it
sorted out the diarrhoea caused by meals
like the watery soup containing a 'bullet'
of meat that prisoners were served on
Wednesdays and Sundays. Secondly, he was
desperate to continue writing about politics
but had nothing except scraps of loo paper
to write on. One of the prison economy's
three valuable commodities, loo paper could
be exchanged for food; Nkrumah willingly
went without food and loo paper.

Even in exile, he maintained a rigid self-
discipline. **Days in Guinea would kick
off with an hour of yoga, and some
grapefruit and cereal with honey.
A late lunch of his favourite meal,
red palm fish stew and fufu (a white,
sticky substance made of cassava)**
after a game of chess or some table tennis,
would be rounded off with a fruit salad and
a few organic vitamin pills, procured for
him by his devoted British secretary from a
shop in Baker Street.

GHANAIAN FISH STEW

Serves 2-3

Kpakpo Shito is a spicy sauce that can be made by blending 12 hot chillies, 2 chopped large ripe tomatoes, 1 chopped onion and salt and pepper together. Palm oil harvesting is leading to the clearing of some of the worlds most valuable forests therefore a substitute of coconut oil is suggested here.

450g/1 lb fresh fish fillets

4 hot chillies pounded to a paste

2 tbsp tomato purée

3 tbsp shrimp powder or paste

4 medium onions, finely sliced

4 fresh tomatoes, chopped and pounded to a paste

6 tbsp Kpakpo Shito

300ml/10fl oz water

150ml/5fl oz red palm oil

1 garlic clove, pounded to a paste

1 tbsp freshly-grated ginger

salt, to taste

Marinate the fish in the garlic, ginger, chillies and salt for 30 minutes before continuing.

Heat a little oil in a pan and fry the onions and tomatoes for a few minutes until softened.

Add the shrimp powder/paste and tomato purée and allow to simmer for about 10 minutes, or until cooked.

Add the water and the marinated fish (along with any remaining marinade) and simmer gently for about 25 minutes, or until the fish is cooked.

Serve with rice or fufu.

ASIA

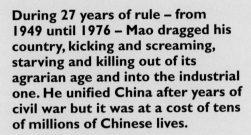

MAO ZEDONG

1893 – 1976

During 27 years of rule – from 1949 until 1976 – Mao dragged his country, kicking and screaming, starving and killing out of its agrarian age and into the industrial one. He unified China after years of civil war but it was at a cost of tens of millions of Chinese lives.

Land reforms, purges of capitalists and political opponents, the Hundred Flowers Campaign, the Great Proletarian Cultural Revolution and the Korean War all contributed to this number. Aside from all these, there were the famous five year plans. He considered his First Five Year such a success that he implemented his Second Five Year Plan (The Great Leap Forward) in 1958 and this, along with drought and flooding, led to the Great Famine. Communes were expected to reach quotas set by the state for production of grain and steel and hand a proportion over to the state. Many communes were left with little food and the only option of melting down utensils to reach target.

Urban life didn't fare better. In Shanghai, citizens would avoid walking on pavements near skyscrapers to miss the falling bodies of those who had committed suicide – their identifiable corpses testament to the authorities that there was no need to persecute the families for defection.

For all his cruel ideological rigidity, Mao was the son of a prosperous Hunan farmer and retained his taste for the finer things in life, making quite sure that he never suffered the privations he forced on his people. **'A revolution is not a dinner party...' was the glib gist of the consolation on offer in his Little Red Book to the millions undergoing the brutal transformation.**

From his earliest years in power, Mao surrounded himself with a personal staff – a cook to feed him, a boy to keep him supplied with water, another to bring him cigarettes, and he was partial to meat-rich European dishes. According to one of his chefs Mao would only allow 20 minutes from ordering until the dish was delivered to his table. There is a record of him once tucking into a whole kilo of stewed beef with a chicken on top. A great delicacy for the Chinese, the *wuhan* fish, was a favourite of his; he once, during a thousand kilometre train journey, ordered that one be kept alive and fresh in an oxygenated plastic bag guarded by an attendant. He hated being served fish that were frozen rather than fresh. **'I will only eat live fish,' he said on a state visit to Stalin before instructing his underlings to insult his host. 'throw these back at them.'**

Later in his rule, a farm grew rice for him alone, its paddies watered by the same spring that had supplied the imperial courts of old China. He had a penchant for rice that was manually husked so that the membrane covering the kernel could be carefully retained. Another farm supplied his vegetables, poultry and dairy products. Only the best tea in China, 'Dragon Well', would do for Mao, and only its best leaves, picked at the best time of day. All his foods were checked by a taster who did duty as his housekeeper too.

In 1968, the 'cult of the mango' sprang up in China. This was unwittingly initiated by Chairman Mao regifting a box of unwanted mangoes from the Pakistani foreign minister. **Mao, not being a fan of fruit and particularly mangoes sent the box to be distributed to Beijing factory workers who were quick to venerate this exotic fruit.** The workers tried to preserve the power of the gifts by coating in wax or drinking the pulp; replicas were made of plastic and wax; mango-decorated mugs and crockery were made; mangoes took centre stage in parades and a poem eulogising the mango written.

All his life, 'the Great Helmsman' was preoccupied by matters of nutrition, digestion and, especially, excretion. While still a young Communist activist, in his early thirties, he would fret that his bowels were only moving once a week. Later, at a time when he was particularly satisfied with his material circumstances, he enthused to a friend in a letter, **'I can eat a lot and shit a lot'.** On a state visit to Moscow to visit Stalin in 1949, he complained bitterly of being constipated due to not feeling relaxed and comfortable enough to use a modern western lavatory, preferring the squatting design. At another point, impatient at having been kept waiting by Stalin he ranted, **'Am I here just to eat, shit and sleep?'**

Personal hygiene seems to have been a special challenge for Mao, though one he did not choose to rise to. His idea of brushing his teeth was a quick rinse with green tea and a chew of the leaves, leading to an unappealing green residue and eventual tooth loss. Consequently in his final years he was only able to eat gum-mashable food, such as stewed bamboo and stir-fried lettuce leaves. In twenty-five years he never had a bath, preferring an occasional rub-down with wet towels by a servant. His ear-holes were greasy and his armpits malodorous, according to one of his many wives who was able to recognise her own long lost son by Mao on account of his sharing both these traits.

A chronic insomniac, Mao would regularly take sleeping pills before dinner and fall asleep in the middle of eating, leaving attendants to fish remaining food from his mouth.

HONG SHAO ROU

Red Braised Pork
Serves 2-3

Ever loyal to his home province of Hunan, Mao's favourite dish was, hong shao rou, a sugary pork-belly confection native to the region, which he ate twice a month in the firm belief that it enhanced his cognitive powers and therefore his ability to trounce his foes. Crucially, the meat had to be that of a Ningxiang pig, an almost thousand year-old breed that has recently been declared an 'agricultural treasure' of the Chinese nation.

450g/ 1lb pork belly

2tbsp peanut oil

25g/ 1oz granulated sugar

1tbsp Shaoxing rice wine or sherry

¾ inch piece of fresh ginger, sliced but with the skin left on

1 star anise

2 dried red chillies

1 small cinnamon stick, or piece of cassia bark

Light soy sauce

1 bunch of spring onions

In just enough water to cover, cook the pork belly in simmering water for 3 to 4 minutes until partially cooked.

Remove and when cool enough to handle cut into bite-sized cubes.

In a hot wok or skillet heat the peanut oil and sugar over a low heat until the sugar has melted. Raise the heat and stir until the sugar caramelises. Plunge the pork belly into a pan of boiling water and simmer for 3 to 4 minutes, until partially cooked. Remove, and when cool enough to handle, cut into bite-size chunks.

Add the pork and toss in the caramelised sugar. Transfer to a large pan and add the wine and enough water to cover the pork belly.

Add the star anise, cinnamon, chillies and ginger. Bring to a gentle boil before turning down the heat and simmering for approximately 1 hour.

As soon as the pork is cooked remove from the heat. Turn the heat back up and reduce the sauce. Season with soy sauce, salt and a little sugar, to taste. Return the pork belly to the pot.

Just before serving, sprinkle the chopped spring onions on top.

Serve with steamed rice.

FERDINAND MARCOS

1917 – 1989

A top lawyer with a photographic memory, Ferdinand Marcos also had the movie star looks and an impressive record fighting the Japanese in World War Two to go far in Filipino politics. Installed as president in 1965, he brushed aside the constitution in 1972, declaring martial law on the pretext of quelling Communist and Muslim insurgencies.

His quintessentially crony capitalist regime was generously supported by the US even after the Marcos' excesses had become too embarrassing to ignore and despite Imelda – the Iron Butterfly – emerging as the real power in the land. In 1986, a rigged election triggered the People Power revolt. The couple were overthrown and fled to exile in Hawaii, where Ferdinand died in 1989.

Unfortunately Imelda was unable to take all of the 3000 shoes and 800 dresses she had amassed and they were later largely destroyed by termites and mould in museum storage. Although they had embezzled between 5 and 10 billion dollars between them, Imelda was amnestied by Ferdinand's successor and, after re-entering Filipino politics in 1991, celebrated her 80th birthday in a hotel in Manila in 2009, in grand old style.

It was in the area of after-dinner entertainment that the Marcos couple excelled. A packed programme of national songs and dances was often embellished by them condescending to croon a duet for their guests.

Ferdinand liked to mark Imelda's birthday banquets by singing her a love song of his own composition. In 1972, on the occasion of Ferdinand's 55th birthday, Imelda

commanded the country's highest ranking military to dress up in drag for the birthday boy; 'every aspect of the occasion was too much, too long and in questionable taste,' the US ambassador at the time sniffily reported back to Washington. Faced with a difficult spouse on a state visit, for example, Imelda went about breaking the ice by introducing a song or a dance. Romania's Elena Ceausescu was reportedly more than usually difficult to engage, but Imelda 'began to hum and then to sing' and soon Mrs Ceausescu was looking at her 'with an expression of interest' and even sang a bar or two herself. In later years, a fashion show was often part of an evening's entertainment.

In their eating habits Ferdinand, at least, was comparatively restrained. He liked nothing better than some broiled fish with boiled vegetables. **Sardines with malunggay, which have a reputation for slowing the ageing process and enhancing the libido – was his favourite dish,**

but he thoroughly enjoyed a rare type of mullet called the 'president's fish' whose distinctive smell and taste make it so desirable it can sell for $114 a kilo. Stir-fried scallops and broccoli as well as deep-fried ribs in salad dressing were also favoured by Ferdinand.

Imelda, however, would only eat what her husband ate when she was on a diet. Mostly, she was true to the dietary customs of the southern region of the country where she hailed from and indulged a hearty appetite and love of fine food. An American insider at the Marcos court has recalled watching her while at lunch at the Indonesian ambassador's fill three whole plates, sampling every one of the buffet dishes.

Perhaps the Indonesian spread was too big a treat to miss because the same American insider observed that the catering arrangements back at Malacanang Palace left a lot to be desired. Catering for the big banquets was always farmed out to various hotels and restaurants, the food arriving at the palace in vans on the morning of a big do. A visiting European chef was shocked to find nothing at all going on in the palace kitchen: **'there was an old Chinese cook asleep in a chair and a cat asleep on the table.'**

Many guests to the palace were regularly irritated by the chaotic situation regarding the serving of alcoholic drinks at functions. Marcos himself was teetotal, but even Imelda would only play with a single glass of white wine; 'the larger the crowd, the fewer waiters and drinks there seemed to be', was how one frequent guest described it. There were rumours that waiters would skimp on opening wine bottles in order to be able to sell the left-over bottles on the black market the following day.

Ferdinand clearly did not much enjoy socialising and was an unsatisfactory conversationalist: 'he talked round questions in astute legalistic circles... a real master of the side-step' was one verdict. Imelda, on the other hand was a party animal and loved nothing better than to show up at her favourite Manila Hotel with up to twenty 'friends' in tow, for a late dinner. Sometimes 'late' would mean 11pm, and the feasting would go on until two or three in the morning. She cleverly combined international missions her husband sent her on with lavish shopping sprees and flitted from parties to discos in whatever country she found herself in. In one of her properties in New York she had a permanent disco ball installed for her lavish parties with live music and luxurious snacks of lobster and steak on offer. **On one trip to Rome she had to reportedly order the pilot of her private plane to turn back because they had forgotten to bring cheese.**

SAUTEED MALUNGGAY & SARDINES

Serves 2 or 3

Malunggay leaves are now recognised as a superfood. Similar to spinach they are a good source of vitamins a, b and c and antioxidants. The health benefits are vast and include strengthening the immune system, preventing intestinal worms, anti-cancer, helping sleep, relieving asthma and headaches.

The Sayote fruit is a pear-shaped green vegetable of the gourd family. It is rich in vitamin c and amino acids.

2 crushed garlic cloves

1 sliced onion

2 Sayote fruit (Chayote) unpeeled and sliced in strips

225g/ 8oz Malunggay (Moringa) leaves

Salt and pepper to taste

2 cans of sardines

Sauté the onion and garlic in a little oil until golden brown. Add the *sayote* and stir fry for a few minutes until it has softened.

Add the sardines, 120 ml of water and the Malunggay leaves. Simmer until the vegetables are dark green but not overcooked.

Season with salt and pepper and serve with rice.

POL POT

1925 – 1998

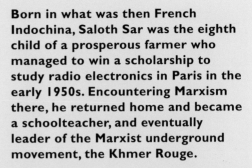

Born in what was then French Indochina, Saloth Sar was the eighth child of a prosperous farmer who managed to win a scholarship to study radio electronics in Paris in the early 1950s. Encountering Marxism there, he returned home and became a schoolteacher, and eventually leader of the Marxist underground movement, the Khmer Rouge.

In 1963 he changed his name to Pol Pot, possibly because it was the abbreviation of the label slapped on him by Chinese Marxists, 'political potential'. By 1975 the Khmer Rouge was a powerful enough force to capture the capital, Pnomh Penh and embark on the speediest and cruellest Communist experiment of all. During the following four years up to quarter of the population died of starvation, torture, disease, overwork or execution. Areas containing the mass graves of people who were buried alive in order to save on the cost of ammunition are now famous as the country's 'Killing Fields'. In 1979, neighbouring Vietnam invaded and pushed Pol Pot and his Khmer Rouge out of Phnom Penh and back into a small jungly area near the Thai border.

Pol Pot, also known as 'the Grand Uncle', died there in 1998, though whether by suicide or by poisoning is not known for certain.

Pol Pot's approach to the implementation of Marx's ideas was thorough in the extreme: the clocks were set back to zero, Phnom Penh's entire population evacuated and relocated to the countryside in order to destroy the old urban elite, and everyone forced into communal living. **All meals were taken in public canteens, which meant that food supplies were easy to control. Two bowls of rice soup, p'baw, a day was the national adult ration.**

As one peasant has recalled, **'We grew rainy season and dry season rice and harvested a lot, but we weren't given any of it to eat. We were only given rice soup – a big pot of water with just a few grains of rice in it.'** Asked how the Communist officials managed on that diet, the same peasant explained, 'They ate with us but then they went home and ate some more. How did we know that? Because we were all thin and they were fat.'

Pol Pot himself – with what one British journalist has described as the 'tapioca-pudding-smooth skin and soft plumpness of a fleshy buddha' – always had plenty to eat and drink, of course, even when in hiding after 1979. According to a former cook, interviewed by the same journalist, he enjoyed 'simple country food' – **venison, wild boar, and even snake, followed by fresh fruit, all washed down with brandy and Chinese wine.**

A recipe for cobra stew which his former cook shared with the journalist has a ring of truth about it. First the cobra must be killed and its head severed from its body. It should then be hung from a tree well out of reach of any children, in order that any poison dries out in the sun. The snake blood should be collected in a cup and served, accompanied by a white wine. Next, the cobra must be chopped into pieces and mashed to a pulp with a handful of peanuts, before being placed in a pot of boiling water with some lemon grass, some bitter vine leaves and some ground ginger, and allowed to simmer for at least an hour.

Small wonder that Pol Pot was plagued by gastric discomfort and found it hard to sleep.

KHMER FISH SALAD

Serves 4

Snakes being a common fact of daily life in the region they feature frequently in the names of food stuffs.

160g/ 6oz snakehead fish, or red snapper fillet

50g/ 2oz finely sliced white cabbage

50g/ 2oz finely shredded purple cabbage

50g/ 2oz shredded iceberg lettuce

a mini cucumber, found in Middle Eastern shops

160g/ 6oz of sliced green pepper

2 finely grated carrots

4 finely sliced shallots

4 snake beans, or a good handful of thin green haricots verts

a handful of bean sprouts

a handful of mint leaves

a handful of Thai basil leaves, or other basil

4tsp sugar

2tsp fish sauce

Lime Marinade

2tsp coriander paste

2 pinches of sliced lemongrass, white part only

240ml/ 8 fl.oz lime juice

Garnish

sliced red chillies

roasted, unsalted peanuts

Combine all the marinade ingredients in a bowl with a pinch of sea salt, and stir until the salt is dissolved

Add the fish and leave it to cure for 10 minutes. Then, squeeze all the marinade out of the fish and set aside, keeping the marinade for later.

Combine all the vegetables and herbs in a large salad bowl.

Add the fish to the salad, along with the sugar, the fish sauce and 120 ml/ 4 fl.oz of the set aside lime marinade. Mix well.

Garnish with roasted, unsalted peanuts and chopped red chillies.

SAPARMURAT NIYAZOV

1940 – 2006

Known as *Turkmenbashi*, meaning 'Chief of all the Turkmen', Turkmenistan's Saparmurat Niyazov got a rotten start in life. His father was killed in World War Two while the rest of the family perished in an earthquake in 1948.

The Communist Party became a second family and he rose quickly through its ranks. His 21-year period of rule – from 1985 until his death in 2006 – spanned the collapse of the Soviet Union to which Turkmenistan belonged, but Niyazov weathered the storm of change. It helped that he and his people were sitting on some of the world's largest natural gas reserves; he could rule as he pleased, usually in a highly eccentric but paternalistic fashion that was not overtly cruel or violent, though it was corrupt and seriously stunted the development of his land and people.

Turkmens saw millions of the country's natural gas-dollars wasted on statues of their dear leader and on a gigantic pink and green illuminated monument to his volume of wisdom, the Ruhnama. They also patiently put up with his random bans on beards, going to the ballet, gold fillings and car radios, as well as punitive travel restrictions, because dissidence to Niyazov was liable to land one in a mental hospital.

'Bodily appetites can cause greediness' is a fair sample of the kind of wisdom contained in Niyazov's *Ruhnama*, his homespun holy book, a mammoth stone replica of which graced the capital, Ashgabat, until his death.

Niyazov was speaking from experience. Brandy was his favourite tipple but he drank it to excess, even while making the haj in Saudi Arabia. **An ex-foreign minister once divulged that he drank so much on his visit to Islam's holiest places that the Saudi king refused to receive him.**

Regular recourse to heroin which is cheap as chips in a land where poppies grow in profusion, reportedly exacerbated his paranoia, causing him to charge around his sprawling residence shooting his pistols at invisible enemies. It took heart by-pass surgery in Munich to put a stop to his drug-taking and that lethal tomfoolery. However, his new-found zeal for health and exercise inspired a decree that all civil servants must walk a 28 kilometre trail in the mountains outside the capital at least once a year. Further folksy health advice included a suggestion that people might improve their dental hygiene and toughen up their teeth as dogs do – by gnawing on bones.

Melons, horsemeat and bread attracted Niyazov's special attention in the nutrition department. He renamed bread Gurbansoltan in memory of his long-lost mother. He also banned the eating of horsemeat on the grounds that the native Akhal Teke breed is so highly prized for its beauty and speed. Every second Sunday in August he declared to be a public holiday in honour of the nation's five hundred varieties of melon.

'Let the life of every Turkmen be as beautiful as our melons!' was Niyazov's ardently expressed wish one melon holiday.

Less healthy options than melons abound in Turkmen cuisine. Chunks of watermelon boiled in a sugar syrup and then mixed with

sheep fat to make a creamy spread known as 'watermelon butter' is a Turkmen breakfast treat. Another artery-clogging favourite is a pilaff. According to popular wisdom the Turkmen version of the staple Central Asian dish needs to be **'so rich that the lamb's fat runs down the eater's arm'.**

PILAFF

Serves 8

Pilaff or Plov, as it is known everywhere in the former Soviet Union, is remarkable for the amount of oil and garlic it requires. The Central Asian answer to barbecue, it is best prepared – usually by men – and eaten al fresco.

1kg/ 2lbs 2oz shoulder or neck of lamb

5 medium carrots

1 large onion

300ml/ 6 fl.oz of cottonseed oil. Vegetable or sunflower oil are good alternatives, never olive oil.

15 cloves of garlic

1.3litre/ 2pts water

1kg/ 2lbs 2oz basmati rice

2 tbsp salt

pepper to taste

Cut the lamb into bite-size chunks. Peel and cut carrots into the shape and size of matchsticks. Peel and slice the onion in half, then slice each half into half rings.

Over a medium flame, heat all the oil – admittedly, a lot – in a large pan with a lid Add the lamb and peeled garlic cloves.

When the meat is browned, add the onion. Add the carrot and cook till soft. Add water and salt and cook for 5 minutes. Add the rice on top. Do not mix in until the end.

Bring to the boil, cover pan and cook for 35-40 minutes.

DICTATORS' DINNERS

KIM JONG-IL

1942 – 2011

The birth of North Korea's 'Dear Leader' heralded the start of an extraordinary chapter in the country's history. His birth was prophesized by a swallow and a double rainbow hung in the sky at that time. A new star was formed in the sky on the night of his birth and from that day on the list of his achievements grew – walking at 3 weeks, talking at 8 weeks and writing operas and copious books.

He was rather short (5ft 2 in) but that was easily rectified with the platform heels and bouffant hair he liked to sport. He had a paunch which was a bit pronounced in his favourite jumpsuit fashion. He had a new golf course built and discovered he was incredibly gifted at it. The first time he picked up a golf club he shot a 38-under-par round, and included 11 holes-in-one. More dictatorial than his father, he decreed a policy of national juche, self-reliance for his country; no more foreign trading, not even with Russia and China. When North Korea was hit by floods and harvests failed, appalling famine ensued. By 1995 people were starving and some 200,000 dissidents languished in prison camps.

Kim Jong-Il admitted to testing a nuclear weapon in 2006 and the US stepped up its sanctions on the country. Included in the list of banned imports to North Korea were yachts and Chanel No 5 – items chosen to try and impact him personally.

Kim Jong-Il beats even his fellow Communist, Cuba's Fidel Castro, to the title of **'The World's Most Foodie Dictator'.**
A true gourmet, he owned a library filled with cookbooks, instructed his ambassadors abroad to send him any local specialities to sample and sent his personal chef jetting all over the world in search of delicacies like Iranian caviar, Danish pork, Thai mangoes and Japanese rice cakes flavoured with mugwort, at $120 a pop.

Hundreds of his luckless people were recruited to the project of preserving his health and vigour by way of his diet. A small army of women was employed to see that every grain of rice destined for his plate was uniform in size, shape and colour. It then had to be cooked over a fire using only trees cut from a mountain peak near the Chinese border. **'This is how you prepare food and water for a god,' one psychologist has observed,**

'Nothing remotely imperfect should pass his lips.' Heaven help anyone who served pizza with anchovy topping.

He had a cellar of 10,000 bottles of fine wine and had around £500,000 worth of finest cognac imported for his personal use each year. Hennessy's biggest customer was reportedly Kim Jong-Il.

Mr Kenji Fujimoto was employed to prepare him the most luxurious sushi in the world: *fugu*, made from the Japanese puffer fish. **In a book revealing all his master's foodie excesses, Fujimoto wrote that Kim Jong-Il 'enjoyed raw fish so fresh that he could start eating it when its mouth was still gasping and its tail still thrashing.'** Live lobsters were airlifted to his train as it crossed Siberia on its way to Moscow. Back home, at an institute whose sole goal was to prolong his life, food was grown for him alone,

while North Koreans starved.

A kind thought of the Dear Leader's in 2006 – a plan to breed giant German rabbits to alleviate the famine – came to nothing, once it was clear that the cost of the feed for the rabbits cancelled out any likely savings on their meat. **In 2000 he 'invented' the gogigyeopbbang – literally, double bread with meat.**

A firm favourite was Shark Fin Soup as well as Poshintang, dog-meat soup which would supposedly provide immunity and virility. Despite being a foodie, Kim Jong-Il would only eat a little of each of the many dishes provided for every meal. He also rather liked Salo (Salted and aged pig fat) and Morning Soup made with mud snails. Perhaps it was his penchant for strong coffee that would ultimately lead to his demise by a heart attack.

SHARK'S FIN SOUP

Serves 6-8

450g/ 1lb shark's fin, about 8 pieces

6 large dried shiitake mushrooms

6 canned bamboo shoots, drained and very finely sliced

225g/ 8oz chicken breast, cooked and shredded

225g/ 8oz small shrimps, cooked and peeled

3 tbsp of Shaoxing rice wine or sherry

4 thin slices of fresh ginger

3 tbsp of peanut oil

3½ pints of chicken stock

2 tbsp cornflour blended with a little water to form a paste

2 tbsp light soy sauce

¼ tsp of ground white pepper

1 tbsp sesame oil

Place the shark fin in a pan and add enough water to just cover it (roughly 2 litres of water). Bring it to the boil and cook, turning the pieces over, for 30 minutes. Drain and cool under cold running water.

Place the boiled shark's fin in a mixing bowl and cover it with cold water. If the shark fin was unskinned clean the surface, remove soft bones, peel the skin and wash with cold water. Let it stand for 24 hours.

Soak the mushrooms in warm water for 30 minutes. Rinse, drain and slice.

Place the cleaned meat in a large pan and add approx 1 litre of water. Bring to the boil and then drain.

Place the meat back in the pan with a further litre of water, the wine and half the ginger. Bring it to the boil and let it simmer for 1 minute. Drain and discard the ginger.

Heat the oil in a wok or skillet and add the bamboo shoots, rest of the ginger and mushrooms. Cook, while stirring, for about 10 seconds. Add the chicken stock and the shark's fin and bring to the boil. Skim off the white foam rising to the surface. Add salt to taste, and the shredded chicken and shrimps. Stir the cornflour paste into the soup.

Add soy sauce, black pepper, sesame oil and serve.

AMERICAS

RAFAEL TRUJILLO

1891 – 1961

Born into a poor family of mixed Haitian and Dominican ancestry, the third of thirteen, Rafael Trujillo was briefly imprisoned for stealing cattle and forging cheques but went on to become a thieving gang leader.

The country's American-formed National Guard was the making of him; after only nine years he was its Commander-in-Chief. He assumed supreme power over the Dominican Republic in 1930. A personality cult saw him compared to Napoleon and Caesar while the capital, a province and a mountain were renamed after him. Even churches were required to sport posters shouting 'Trujillo on Earth and God in Heaven'. Privately, he was known as Chapitas (Bottlecaps, on account of all the medals he awarded himself) or El Chivo (the Goat, in a reference to his voracious sexual appetite).

Although he improved the country's infrastructure and industry, Trujillo's ownership of 60% of the republic's arable land and 80% of that industry made him fabulously wealthy. Profoundly racist, he discriminated against and persecuted dark-skinned Haitians while welcoming any white-skinned Europeans to settle in the republic, including 10,000 Jewish refugees after World War Two. He was assassinated in 1961, while en route to visit one of his many mistresses.

Rafael Trujillo was a heady mixture of the masculine and the feminine – a cross between Rudolf Valentino and Imelda Marcos perhaps.

Along with a ludicrously high-pitched voice and a love of the pancake make-up he wore to disguise his swarthy Haitian ancestry, he owned over 2,000 suits and uniforms, 10,000 ties and 500 pairs of shoes. On the other hand, his predatory sexual appetite – a taste for plump young virgins – was legendary. As one close associate has recalled, **'In the modern world no other man relieved women of their virginities with greater frequency than he did.'** The fathers of well-born teenage girls strove to keep them out of his sight, knowing that a refusal to let El Chivo (The Goat) have his wicked way could mean job loss or even imprisonment.

Virgins on a plate were Trujillo's favourite delicacy. Food does not **seem to have excited him in the same way.** Not for Trujillo the average dictator's faddiness or digestive disorders. He kept himself trim and healthy with a clockwork routine that entailed a light, early breakfast, a large lunch at noon followed by a two kilometre walk, a ninety-minute siesta, a light supper and precisely half an hour with his aged mother.

Exemplary. Quite unlike his dinner table conversation. With advancing age, he drank more and, when deep in his cups, his alley cat origins re-surfaced, along with a hot temper. Abusive language included words like pendejo – literally, pubic hair, but popularly, idiot or motherfucker. **Always anxious to be accepted as upper class, Trujillo affected to like European cuisine but actually preferred his native Creole food.**

Native versus European, dark or pale, Dominican or Haitian were crucial distinctions for him. The atrocity for which he is remembered – a massacre of up to 20,000 Haitians in 1937 – is known as the Parsley Massacre. His troops sorted darker-skinned Haitians from Dominicans by dangling a sprig of parsley before each and asking them what it was. If the person proved unable to say *perejil* with a grandly rolled 'r' he was hacked to death with machetes.

Parsley features in a national dish, a stew containing seven different kinds of meat.

SANCOCHO DOMINICANO DE SIETE CARNES

Serves 8

A sancocho de siete carnes is a feature of any Dominican celebration – baptisms, weddings, birthdays – usually accompanied by cold beer or rum.

450g/ 1lb each of stewing beef, goat meat, Dominican pork sausage, stewing pork, chicken, spare ribs, smoked ham off the bone

2 lemons

1 tsp dried parsley

½ tsp powdered oregano

1 tbsp chopped garlic

1 ½ tsp salt

4 tbsp vegetable oil

2.5 litres/ 5 pints water

230g/ 5oz sliced yam

230g/ 5oz yautia – starchy brown tuber, eaten like yam or potato

230g/ 5oz cassava, chopped small

3 green bananas, 2 of them chopped in rings of 2 ½ cm

2 corn cobs, cut in rings of 2 ½ cm

Cut all meat into bite-size chunks. Cover all meat, except the sausage, in the lemon juice.

Heat the vegetable oil in a heavy casserole pan over a medium flame. Add the beef and stir. Cover and cook for 10 minutes. (Add water by the spoonful at any stage if the mixture seems about to burn).

Add pork and stir. Cover and cook for 15 minutes.

Add the rest of the meat and cook for another 5 minutes. Add 2L of water. When it starts to boil add the yam, cassava and chopped bananas. Cook covered for 15 minutes. Add all other ingredients and cook, stirring frequently.

Add salt to taste and serve with rice.

'PAPA DOC'

1907 – 1971

After studying medicine in the United States, François Duvalier was affectionately nicknamed Papa Doc by grateful patients whom he treated in the poor rural regions of Haiti.

He was already fifty when, dressed in a dark suit and thick spectacles and speaking up boldly for black Haitians against the haughty mulatto elite who dominated Haiti, he was elected president. But he aimed at being first a 'strong man' and then a god. During his 14-year reign, but especially from 1959 until his death, he presided over a terror state. His paramilitary force, the infamous Tonton Macoutes in their uniform straw hats, denim shirts and mirror sunglasses, was twice the size of Haiti's army.

By the early 1960s, wearing a black tail coat, homburg and sunglasses and with a high nasal voice, Papa Doc was the incarnation of the powerful voodoo spirit of crossroads, Baron Samedi. By the time he died, the Tontons Macoutes were accounting for half the national budget and tens of thousands of Haitians had fled the country. It has been estimated that some 30,000 Haitians were shot, imprisoned or tortured to death during his era. 'Grim but courteous' was Alan Whicker's verdict on the man who was succeeded by his son, 'Baby Doc'.

'**What is in your stomach is what's yours**' and '**Hunger is misery but a full stomach is trouble**' are two popular Haitian proverbs which together testify to centuries of miserable poverty and cruel misgovernment. But never before or since has it been as dangerous, surreal and crazily blasphemous, as in the era of Papa Doc. He even re-wrote the Lord's Prayer, substituting himself and Haiti for the Christian God.

'Our Doc, who art in the National Palace for life, hallowed be thy name by present and future generations. Thy will be done in Port-au-Prince, as it is in the provinces. Give us this day our new Haiti and forgive not the trespasses of those anti-patriots who daily spit on our country...'

Formally Roman Catholic but informally firmly wedded to a belief in Voodoo, Haitians were easily terrorised into believing that their leader not only dressed like the Voodoo spirit Baron Samedi but was him, and therefore requiring of placatory ceremonies featuring regular and plentiful animal sacrifices, especially of chickens and goats. For good measure, every voodoo temple in Haiti housed a picture of the president and the licence plates on his official car bore the number 22, Baron Samedi's number.

It seems highly unlikely that Papa Doc ever ate a fraction of the mountains of animal flesh sacrificed for him. Slight and frail and always older-looking than his years, he was already a diabetic requiring daily shots of insulin by the time he became president. Afflicted by heart disease, he suffered so badly from arthritis in his wrist that he found it hard to lift a telephone receiver, and popped pills for the constant pain. In the year before he died, unable to chew any food, he relied on his wife to spoon-feed him and massage his jaw.

There are many who believe that a heart attack he suffered two years after gaining power was what accounted for his dramatic character change; increasingly paranoid, he reportedly began ranting like Hitler. **His idea of after-dinner entertainment involved a descent to a dungeon whose walls were painted a blood red, to watch through a spy-hole while his enemies were being tortured.**

POULET CREOLE

Serves 8

The Scotch bonnet chilli gives this northern Haitian dish a good, violent kick.

1.8kg/ 4lb chicken, cut into 8 portions

3 garlic cloves

3 roughly chopped spring onions

a handful of chopped parsley

a sprig of fresh thyme

1 Scotch bonnet chilli

1 green pepper, thinly sliced

2 tbsp vegetable oil

1 large onion, thinly sliced

half a red pepper, thinly sliced

2 tbsp tomato purée

Arrange the chicken in a shallow baking dish.

Food-process the garlic, the Scotch bonnet, half the green pepper and ½ pint of water. Pour it over the chicken and put in fridge for at least 4 hours, then scrape off the marinade and set aside.

Using a heavy-bottomed pan, heat some oil and brown the chicken on all sides for about 10 minutes. Remove from the pan and set aside.

Add the onions, the other half of the green pepper, the red pepper and salt and pepper to the pot. Cook until soft, for about 10 minutes.

Return the chicken to the pot, with the marinade and a pint of water. Bring to the boil.

Reduce the heat to low and half-cover the pot, stirring from time to time, for 25 to 30 minutes.

ALFREDO STROESSNER

1912 – 2006

Paraguay's General Alfredo Stroessner was the son of an immigrant Bavarian brewer and a Paraguayan belle. El Tyrannosaur, as he was known to his opponents, rose to power through the ranks of the military, becoming the youngest general in South America by 1948. Six years later he was in sole control of the only two institutions that counted in Paraguay: the army and the conservative Colorado Party.

Paraguay became a contraband state, with the wholesale smuggling of drugs, arms, car parts and whisky accounting for much of its economy. The early years of his regime were the most brutal. Over 400 dissidents were killed or 'disappeared' on his watch, the longest period of rule South America has ever seen. Faithful to his German antecedents, Stroessner had his army march in goose-step and disgusted international opinion by sheltering the SS doctor at Auschwitz, Jozef Mengele, and possibly also top Nazi official, Martin Bormann.

After first supporting Stroessner as a reliable bulwark against Communism in the region, the US gradually stopped its annual aid payments. He was removed by his son-in-law in a military coup in 1989; it was feared that he was grooming either his drug addicted son Freddie, or his homosexual son Gustavo to succeed him.

General Stroessner seems to have
ranked his German above his Paraguayan
roots. Spartan living conditions, a smart
appearance, featuring tailored uniforms
embellished with multiple medals,
punctuality, fitness and self-discipline were
joined with a paternalism demonstrated by
stunts like ordering free breakfasts for all
the municipal workers in the Asuncion park
where he liked to take his morning walk.

**There were compensating vices,
however. Hypocrisy, for one. Although
carrying more than a few extra kilos
of paunch himself thanks to his love
of Paraguay's highly calorific cuisine,
he would not tolerate obesity in
others.** A journalist was commanded to
lose weight and members of his security
forces learned to avoid his line of vision if
they were on the chubby side.

Stroessner's rankest hypocrisy however, was in the area of underage sex. Although married to Dona Eligia, by whom he had three children, he fathered fifteen more, many of them by girls he selected for his personal delectation while they were still at school. He would have his chauffeur park his car outside the school gates at lunch-time and make his selection from its back seat before instructing an underling to see to the necessary arrangements.

One mistress, of eighteen years standing, was a 15 year-old schoolgirl when he first encountered her in 1960, at a lunch given by a relative. He was 48, but his wooing of her progressed from messages delivered to her at school by one of his guards, to unannounced teatime visits to her home, to inviting himself to stay to dinner, to sending a chauffeur to take her to and from school. **With Nata and their two illegitimate daughters he played at being Juan Average, reportedly liking nothing better than to shop for food at a supermarket and cook his little family a meal.**

Unfortunately, there is no record of what he liked to cook them, but it might well have included the national staple, *sopa paraguaya* – not a soup, as the name suggests, but a form of calorie-crammed quiche. **It is possible that, in a respectful nod to the old Fatherland, he garnished it with a grilled pork sausage or two.**

SOPA PARAGUAYA

Serves 4-6

A country whose national dish is a solid soup – I don't want to begin to imagine what the rest of it is like...' Gabriel Garcia Marquez.

110g/ 25oz butter

1 large onion

225g/ 8oz cottage cheese

110g/ 4oz grated mild cheese, preferably a German one, like Munster

300g/ 10oz cornmeal

400g/ 14oz sweet corn

240ml milk

1 tsp salt

6 eggs, separated

Melt half the butter and fry the onions until they are soft, but not brown. Set aside.

Combine the rest of the softened butter with the cottage cheese.

Add the mild cheese, chopped onion, cornmeal, sweetcorn, salt, milk and egg yolks. Mix thoroughly.

Beat the egg whites until they form soft peaks, and fold into the batter.

Pour the batter into a greased and floured baking tin (25cm by 30cm). Bake at 200 degrees centigrade, for 45 to 55 minutes.

167

DICTATORS' DINNERS

FIDEL CASTRO

b.1926

The bourgeois son of a Spanish immigrant, Fidel Castro ruled Cuba from 1959 until 2008 when, aged 84, he handed over to his brother Raul. The leader of the only Marxist-Leninist state in the western hemisphere, Castro was an irritatingly charismatic thorn in the side of generations of American presidents.

All efforts to assassinate him – from trying to poison one of his cigars and his scuba diving suit, to co-opting the Mafia, to filling a biro with a hypodermic syringe of poison – failed. 'If surviving assassination attempts were an Olympic event, I would win the gold medal,' Castro once boasted. Decades of economic blockade, counter-revolutionary agitation and even invasion in the famously failed Bay of Pigs operation did not dislodge, let alone kill him. In 1962, Castro's willingness to try the US's patience by agreeing to the siting of Soviet nuclear weapons on Cuba could have ended in global annihilation; the world came closer to the brink of nuclear war than ever before.

But the demise of the USSR in 1991 spelt the end of Soviet subsidies for Cuba and the US's interminable Tom and Jerry contest with Cuba began to wane. In 2009 President Obama lifted restrictions on travel and émigré Cubans were permitted to send remittances home.

Long before Jamie Oliver, a youthful Fidel Castro was extolling the virtues of plain, fresh ingredients and invading outraged women in their kitchens to instruct them in the proper art of cooking lamb cutlets, salted cod, spaghetti or fried bananas: **…'the best thing is not to boil the shrimp or lobster... Lobster takes eleven minutes to bake or six minutes on a skewer over hot coals. Baste only with butter, garlic and lemon. Good food is simple food.'**

Food and drink has been a passion for the western world's leading Communist, with a lot of effort and money wasted on pet projects like setting up enterprises to produce French cheese, foie gras and whisky. Even his daughter recalls that some of the little time he spent with her was wasted on explaining how to roast pumpkin seeds by grilling them 'on a slow flame until the shells almost come off by themselves…' He would drop by her mother's home unannounced bearing black market delicacies at a time when grim jokes about starvation were in vogue: **'What's the difference between a Cuban fridge and a coconut? Nothing, they both contain water';** a sign in the national zoo had to be changed from reading **'Do not feed the animals'**, to **'Do not eat the animal feed'**, to **'Do not eat the animals.'**

Cuban state media was publicising some innovative serving suggestions to ease the situation. One recipe featured mashed potatoes and onions, garnished with pork fat and orange juice. Another recommended a pudding of potatoes, sugar and orange peel.

Aged seventy-eight in 2004, Castro was still meddling in kitchen affairs, urging every Cuban woman to invest in a Chinese pressure cooker at the cost of approximately half the average household's monthly income. When he resigned his duties as leader to his brother Raul in 2008 to undergo surgery on his intestines, Castro's personal physician bullishly reckoned that he could live until he was 140.

His loyal comrade in the struggle and possibly one-time lover, **Celia Sanchez, has revealed that a much younger Castro was particularly fond of a soup made from an endangered and now internationally protected species – the turtle.**

TURTLE SOUP

Serves 4-6

*The freshwater snapper turtle is a viable
alternative to the protected sea turtle, but
oxtail, veal or beef are also useful substitutes.*

250g / 9oz unsalted butter
75g/ 3oz of plain flour
1.4kg/ 3lbs turtle meat, or substitute
4 celery stalks
2 minced onions
1½tsp minced garlic
3 bay leaves
1 tsp oregano
½tsp thyme
½ tsp fresh ground black pepper
300g/ 10oz of tomato puree
1l/ 340fl.oz beef stock
120ml/ 4fl.oz lemon juice
5 hard-boiled eggs
parsley
6 tsp of dry sherry
salt and pepper

Thoroughly wash the meat under cold
running water and drain. Remove any bones
and cut into half-inch cubes.

Melt 200g butter in a heavy casserole.

Add the flour and cook over medium heat,
stirring frequently, until the roux is light
brown, and then set aside.

In a large saucepan melt 50g of butter. Add
the meat and cook over high heat until
browned. Add celery, onions, garlic and
seasonings and cook until the vegetables
are transparent. Add tomato purée.

Lower heat and simmer for 30 minutes.

Add the roux and cook over low heat until
the soup is smooth and thickened. Season
with salt and pepper. Add the lemon juice,
sliced eggs and parsley.

Remove from heat and serve, adding 1tsp of
sherry to each plate.